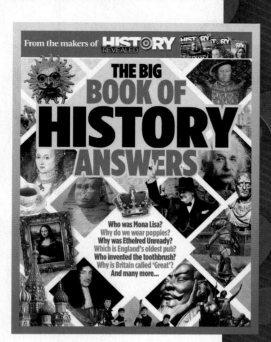

# Welcome

For a subject that covers the entirety of human existence, it's unsurprising that history can be home to the odd half-truth. And that's where *The Big Book Of History Answers* comes in – busting myths and fixing fallacies from across the centuries.

From the Romans to Remembrance Day, Boudicca to The Beatles, we shed **fresh light on every corner of history**. Thanks to the deep knowledge and wisdom of our panel of eggheads, you yourself can become an instant expert on all manner of subjects, making you the envy of your friends, family and pub quiz team. What did **Hitler do during World War I**? How did they **build the Colosseum**? And just what did happen to **Einstein's brain**?

And we don't just tackle the big questions. The devil is in the detail, whether it's providing the definitive word on how **sideburns got their name**, evaluating the **worst jobs in Tudor England** or deducing who received **the world's first speeding ticket**. You'll never be left in the dark again.

This **expert testimony** is culled from the pages of *History Revealed*, the monthly magazine that brings the past to life. So, if you want answers to **historical conundrums** on a regular basis, turn to page 114 where you'll find full details of how to subscribe.

**Paul McGuinness**
Editor

## OUR EXPERTS

 **EMILY BRAND** Historian, genealogist and author of *Mr Darcy's Guide To Courtship*

 **JULIAN HUMPHRYS** Development Officer for The Battlefields Trust and author

 **GREG JENNER** *Horrible Histories* consultant and author of *A Million Years in a Day*

 **SANDRA LAWRENCE** Writer and columnist specialising in British heritage subjects

 **SEAN LANG** Senior Lecturer in History at Anglia Ruskin University and author

 **RUPERT MATTHEWS** Author on a range of historical subjects, from ancient to modern

 **MILES RUSSELL** Author and Senior Lecturer in Archaeology at Bournemouth University

Bringing the past to life

**EDITORIAL**
**Editor** Paul McGuinness
paul.mcguinness@historyrevealed.com
**Production Editor** Mel Sherwood
mel.sherwood@historyrevealed.com
**Staff Writer** Jonny Wilkes
jonny.wilkes@historyrevealed.com
**Editorial contributor** Nige Tassell

**ART**
**Art Editor** Sheu-Kuei Ho
**Designer** Jane Gollner
**Picture Editor** Rosie McPherson
**Illustrators** Tidy Design

**PRESS & PR**
**Communications Manager**
Dominic Lobley 020 7150 5015
dominic.lobley@immediate.co.uk

**ADVERTISING & MARKETING**
**Advertisement Manager**
Sam Jones 0117 314 8847
sam.jones@immediate.co.uk
**Brand Sales Executive**
Sam Evanson 0117 314 8754
sam.evanson@immediate.co.uk
**Subscriptions Director**
Jacky Perales-Morris
**Marketing Executive** Natalie Medler

**CIRCULATION**
**Circulation Manager** Helen Seymour

**PRODUCTION**
**Production Director** Sarah Powell
**Production Co-ordinator**
Emily Mounter
**Ad Co-ordinator** Jade O'Halloran
**Ad Designer** Rachel Shircore
**Reprographics** Rob Fletcher,
Tony Hunt, Chris Sutch

**PUBLISHING**
**Publisher** David Musgrove
**Publishing Director** Andy Healy
**Managing Director** Andy Marshall
**Chairman** Stephen Alexander
**Deputy Chairman** Peter Phippen
**CEO** Tom Bureau

**To become a subscriber to**
*History Revealed,* please turn
to page 114 for details of our
latest subscription offer

ALAMY X6, GETTY X7, DREAMSTIME X2, ISTOCK X3

# CONTENTS

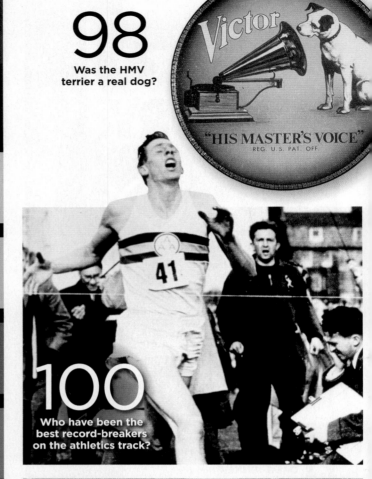

**98**
Was the HMV terrier a real dog?

"HIS MASTER'S VOICE"
REG. U.S. PAT. OFF.

**100**
Who have been the best record-breakers on the athletics track?

**20**
Who were the Huns?

**63**
Which battle had the highest death toll ever?

**46**
Was Isaac Newton, Britain's greatest physicist, a religious man?

# THE BIG BOOK OF HISTORY ANSWERS

## 88
How did the Black Prince get his name?

## 83
Why did Charles II take out an advert in the paper?

## 24
Why did eating jellied eels go out of fashion?

## 56
What is a quizzing glass?

## 104
How did the Romans build the Colosseum?

## WONDERS OF THE WORLD

## 12
How was the Great Sphinx carved from one piece of limestone?

## 58
The beguiling statues of Easter Island

# IS THIS THE SHAPE OF THINGS TO COME?

It may look like a prototype design for the robot from 1950s science-fiction cult movie *Forbidden Planet*, but this is actually a diving suit. Designed by engineer Joseph Salim Peress (seen here demonstrating his creation at the 1925 Shipping, Engineering and Machinery Exhibition at Olympia), the stainless steel suit will, he claims, allow divers to reach great depths while at atmospheric pressure. Steel proves way too heavy to be used underwater, but an undeterred Peress goes on to pioneer the first practical diving suit in 1930.

# WHAT'S THE BIG RUSH?

At high noon on 22 April 1889, the sound of the cavalry bugle rings out across the empty lands of modern-day Oklahoma. By sundown, Oklahoma City will not only have been founded, but will have a population of 10,000.

The Native American tribes who called this land home have been removed in anticipation of this 'land rush', in which an estimated 50,000 people race into the two million-acre Unassigned Lands to secure their own plot and develop it. These 'Boomers' are allowed to claim 160 acres each, unless the 'Sooners' – people who had illegally entered the land early – claim them first.

# WHAT ARE THESE WOMEN MAKING?

In 1966, and with meticulous precision, employees of North American Aviation toil away on the components of a NASA module, to be used in the Apollo program.

The work of the aerospace company proved vital to American success in the Space Race, as they were responsible for helping develop the Saturn V rockets, as well as various Apollo command and service modules. A year after this photo was taken, however, NAA faced severe criticism after the Apollo 1 tragedy, when the command module burst into flames during a test run, killing the three astronauts inside.

## HOW DID THEY DO THAT?
# THE GREAT SPHINX

One of the largest and oldest monolithic statues in the world, the Sphinx continues to keep watch over the Great Pyramids

With the body of a lion and the head of a human, the Great Sphinx, in the Giza Plateau in Egypt, was carved from a single mass of limestone nearly 5,000 years ago. Although the history of the 73-metre-long colossus is steeped in mystery, it is believed to have been constructed during the reign of Pharaoh Khafre – who also built the second of the Great Pyramids – and may bear the ruler's likeness. The Sphinx is a seminal part of Egypt today, attracting millions of tourists every year, as well as a link to the land's ancient civilisation.

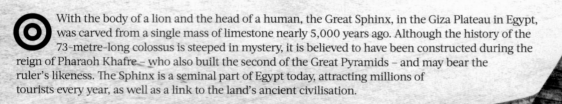

### RED-FACED
There are clues to the Great Sphinx's original appearance. Residue of red pigment was found, so it is possible the whole face used to be dark red.

### A CLOSE SHAVE
When the Sphinx was excavated, fragments of a stone plaited beard were found. It is unlikely to have been part of the original carving, but added some 1,000 years later.

### BURIED BODY
All the Sphinx, apart from the head, was buried in sand for thousands of years. The excavation was began by Italian explorer Giovanni Battista Caviglia in 1817, but the body wasn't cleared until the 20th century.

### THE DREAM STELA
Between the paws of the Sphinx is a large slab, the Dream Stela, which was erected by Thutmose IV (who reigned 1401-1391 BC) after he ordered restoration work on the statue. It relates a dream Thutmose had as a prince, in which the Sphinx offered him the throne in return for his help rebuilding its body.

## WHAT HAPPENED TO THE NOSE OF THE GREAT SPHINX?

The most-repeated legend tells how soldiers in Napoleon's army used the Sphinx for target practice and blew off the nose with a cannonball, but this has been dismissed as illustrations predating Napoleon's time show the statue to be nose-less. A 15th-century document attributes the destruction to a Sufi Muslim named Muhammad Sa'im al-Dahr, who was angered that peasants were making offerings to the Sphinx. He was allegedly executed c1378 for vandalism after attacking the statue and destroying the nose.

It was during Napoleon's Egypt campaign that the Rosetta Stone was discovered, and the legend that his soldiers destroyed the Sphinx's nose began

### PHARAOH'S FACE
Although a hotly debated subject, it is generally accepted that the face of the Sphinx depicts Pharaoh Khafre himself, who is buried in one of the nearby pyramids of Giza.

### LEFT OVERS
Due to the Great Sphinx's position in a deep pit away from the pyramids, it is thought that it was carved in a limestone quarry used for the construction of the Pyramid of Khafre.

### PASSAGE OF TIME
The body of the Sphinx, which is of a softer limestone, has eroded more than the head, but it was protected while buried in sand.

20m

73m     20m

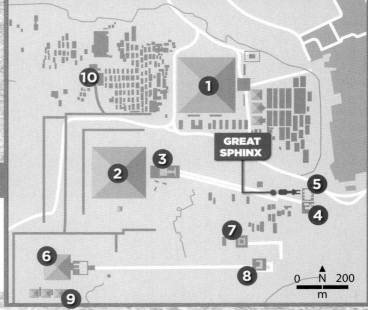

GREAT SPHINX

0   N   200
        m

## GIZA NECROPOLIS

1. Pyramid of Khufu
2. Pyramid of Khafre
3. Mortuary Temple of Khafre
4. Valley Temple of Khafre
5. Temple of the Sphinx
6. Pyramid of Menkaure
7. Tomb of Queen Khentkawes
8. Valley Temple of Menkaure
9. The Queen's Pyramids
10. Tomb of Hemon

## THROUGH THE AGES
The Sphinx has attracted explorers, historians and artists from all over Europe and through their work, we can trace the erosion of the statue

| 1610 | 1698 | 1737 | 1798 | 1839 | 1858 | 1887 | 1925 |
|------|------|------|------|------|------|------|------|
| George Sandys | Cornelis de Bruijn | Frederic Norden | Vivant Denon | David Roberts | Francis Frith | Henri Béchard | Émile Baraize |

# THE ANCIENT WORLD

## DID THE ROMANS FEEL THE COLD ON HADRIAN'S WALL?

### DID YOU KNOW?

**VICTORY CRY**

In 368 BC, the Spartans faced the Arcadians in battle. According to legend, the Spartan army advanced on its enemy, halted, then let rip with its deafening battle cry. Terrified, the entire Arcadian army promptly turned and fled.

The wall wasn't manned by shivering Italians; it was largely guarded by non-Roman auxiliaries from across the Empire, including modern-day Belgium and the Netherlands, where the weather could be equally chilly. The houses of garrison commanders were equipped with underfloor heating, and we know from writing tablets found at Vindolanda fort that soldiers on the wall were sent woolly socks and underpants, and wore a variety of cloaks. Those who could afford one splashed out on a long, hooded cloak known as a 'birrus Britannicus'. These were made from untreated wool, so they kept the rain out as well as the cold. Large numbers of them were exported from Britain to use in other parts of the Roman Empire.

**FREEZING FRONTIER**
Hadrian's Wall in winter wasn't the place for Mediterranean types

GETTY X3, THINKSTOCK X1

# What was the Byzantine Empire?

◎ Modern historians use this name for the eastern Roman empire, which survived the barbarian migrations that tore apart the west in the fifth century AD. By the ninth century, it had become a more medieval and overtly Christian state than the more 'Roman' entity that preceded it. In his 1557 work *Corpus Historiae Byzantinae*, the German historian Hieronymus Wolf crystallised the distinction by coining the term 'Byzantine', from the Ancient Greek name for its capital city, Constantinople (now Istanbul).

## 250,000

The capacity of the Circus Maximus, Rome's premier chariot-racing track. This figure is more than a third of the city's population.

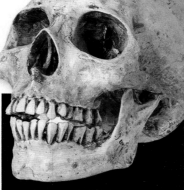

**FLAT EARTH**
In medieval times, many people still believed the world was flat

## DID THE CELTS PRACTISE HUMAN SACRIFICE?

◎ According to the Romans, the answer is "yes, lots". It was one of the reasons they gave for suppressing druidic cults in France and Britain. Rome was not averse to human sacrifice in the arena (for entertainment's sake), but was against it being conducted for religious reasons. This could be just Roman propaganda, were it not for evidence from the bogs of northern Europe that suggests violent death was a key part of Celtic life.

## DID THE ANCIENTS KNOW THE WORLD WAS ROUND?

◎ Some of them certainly did. Greek philosophers were debating the shape and nature of Earth as long ago as the sixth century BC and, although the 'circular Earth theory' is credited to the mathematician Pythagoras, most well-educated members of Hellenistic society were in agreement that the planet was spherical.

In the mid-third century BC, philosopher and mathematician Eratosthenes took this concept further and, after studying the angle of shadows cast at the summer solstice in his home city of Alexandria, calculated that Earth had a circumference of 250,000 stades. Sadly, the precise length of a 'stade' is unknown, although modern mathematicians suggest that his figure contained an error of less than 16 per cent.

# DID CRASSUS DIE FROM DRINKING MOLTEN GOLD?

**In 55 BC, Marcus Licinius Crassus, the wealthiest man in Rome, needed a military victory to consolidate his grip on power. His campaign against the eastern Parthian Empire started well enough, but at Carrhae in Turkey the Romans were comprehensively defeated and Crassus killed. It's not known whether he died fighting or** committed suicide to prevent capture, but later historian Cassius Dio wrote that, having discovered his body, the enemy "poured molten gold into his mouth in mockery for he had set great store by money". Where Dio got this information isn't known, but it helped confirm Roman prejudices about Parthian brutality.

# WHY DID HIPPOCRATES EAT EARWAX?

**Often dubbed the Father of Medicine, Hippocrates of Kos (c460–375 BC) came from a family of doctors and underwent the usual training at the local 'asclepeion' temple – where priests treated the sick using religious magic, dream interpretation and snake-worship.**

Yet, Hippocrates rejected such supernatural causality and argued for a rational, bodily explanation for illnesses. His belief was that the body had four 'humours' – black bile, yellow bile, blood and phlegm – and that these fitted into a sort of elemental Venn diagram of hot, cold, wet and dry. Disease was the result of imbalances in these elements caused by diet, climate and living habits, and had nothing to do with meddling gods.

But how did he diagnose what ailed a patient? Well, he advocated the analysis of urine, faeces, pus, mucus, vomit, sweat and earwax, and was even prepared to taste some of them. He suggested bitter earwax was a sign of good health, but sweet wax was cause for alarm.

Humourism was dominant in medicine until well into the mid-19th century, giving rise to many stories of blood-lettings, purgative vomits, and seemingly barbaric treatments dished out to peasants and princes alike. But Hippocrates had actually been a cautious, gentle doctor and had vigorously demanded high standards of ethics from his followers, which is why modern doctors honour his name by taking a Hippocratic Oath to do no harm.

# When did the Roman Empire end?

**This depends on your definition of 'Roman', 'Empire' and 'ended'.** Some say it was in AD 410, when the city of Rome was taken by Alaric the Goth. Alaric, however, did not want to finish Rome, so the city survived, but no longer thrived. A second 'sack' occurred in AD 455, when the Vandals, a Germanic tribe, appeared. The Vandals, however, had been invited to Rome to help the widow of the previous emperor. They left Rome intact, but they did empty the state coffers.

New emperors were created (and deposed) until 4 September AD 476, when the last, Romulus 'Augustulus', was forced to retire by Odoacer, a German who became king. By now, most of the western provinces of the Empire had been taken by various tribes, most of whom perpetuated Roman language and culture. A 'rump-state' comprising the province of Dalmatia (in the Balkans) survived until AD 480, when this too was finally absorbed into Odoacer's kingdom. The eastern half of the Empire continued until the capture, by Ottoman armies, of its capital, Constantinople, in 1453. Some pockets of 'Roman' power survived until the 15th century, such as at Trebizond on the Turkish Black Sea coast.

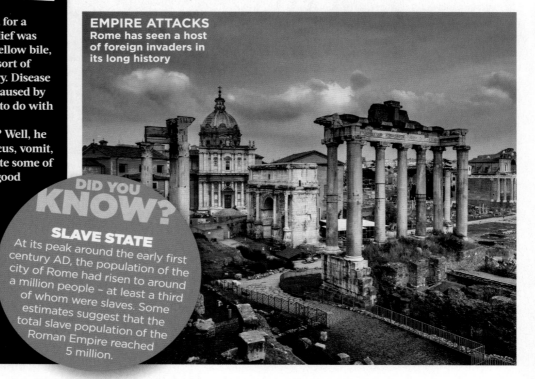

**EMPIRE ATTACKS**
Rome has seen a host of foreign invaders in its long history

**DID YOU KNOW?**

**SLAVE STATE**
At its peak around the early first century AD, the population of the city of Rome had risen to around a million people – at least a third of whom were slaves. Some estimates suggest that the total slave population of the Roman Empire reached 5 million.

**SITE OF CELEBRATION**
Druids gather at the sacred Wiltshire site to celebrate the winter solstice. But for how long have they done so?

# DID THE DRUIDS HAVE ANYTHING TO DO WITH STONEHENGE?

Archaeology has shown that Stonehenge began as an earthwork and cremation cemetery in around 3100 BC, with its final phases of construction ending in the Bronze Age, around about 1600 BC. That puts its completion at more than a millennium before the first historical references to Druids in the writings of Greek and Roman historians. However, the stones were set up for ritual and religious purposes and they remained accessible for every generation since the Neolithic period. With that in mind, it is highly unlikely that Druid priests of the Celtic Iron Age and Roman period did not worship or make offerings there, much as people still do today.

## DID YOU KNOW?

**ADDING FLAVOUR**
'Salary' comes from the Latin for salt. Roman soldiers were paid 'salt money' - an essential in hot, sweaty climates. By the Middle Ages, the word 'salary' was being used to mean any sort of pay – regardless of what you spent it on.

## WHAT'S THE OLDEST CHAT-UP LINE IN HISTORY?

If there's one thing we learn from historical seduction guides, it's that there isn't much new under the sun. Early-modern suggestions for chatting up a woman include blatant flattery, offering beer and cheesecake, suggesting you might relieve her of the 'burden' of virginity and comparing her belly to Salisbury Plain. Perhaps the oldest guide to romance is Ovid's tongue-in-cheek *The Art of Love* (c2 AD) and much of it seems familiar. Men of Ancient Rome are advised to hang out at the theatre or the chariot race, and start conversation with a lady about the spectacle or who she supports. They are encouraged to declare a passion while drunk (so it can be retracted later) but, if all else fails, simply to go for melodrama – women long to hear a man is "dying of a frantic passion" or the simple words: "You're the only girl for me."

**Seduction techniques from history remain familiar today**

## HAVE PEOPLE EVER LIVED UNDERGROUND?

The best example of possible subterranean living is an impressive system of tunnels and passageways in central Turkey. The precise origin of the underground city of Derinkuyu – as well as who dug the passages and when – are unclear, but major excavation activity has suggested the city could be as old as the eighth century BC.

The multi-layered Derinkuyu reaches a depth of 85 metres and could shelter some 20,000 people. The passageways have been periodically enlarged and extended with multiple areas for accommodation, storage and also defence. No written testimony exists explaining how the city was used, although it has been claimed the tunnels were conceived as a combination of cold storage facilities and ancient underground bunker, protecting the population during times of invasion or internal strife. That so few of the passageways and rooms have been investigated serves to make Derinkuyu even more alluring and mysterious.

# When were coins first made?

**SPARE CHANGE**
The silver coin depicts the god Apollo while the gold coins show animals, including a lion

The very earliest coins were pieces of precious metal that were stamped with a design to guarantee their purity and weight. It is thought that the first coins were produced in the mid 500s BC in Asia Minor. Local rulers had to pay Greek mercenaries a set weight of precious metal at the end of their contracts, and to ensure the correct amount was paid, coins were used. These pieces of metal were generally stamped with an animal head on one side, perhaps indicating the person who issued them, and an abstract design on the other signifying the weight.

The first coins to be issued with the intention that they would be used as money were those minted by King Croesus of Lydia, a rich and powerful Greek state on the west coast of what is now Turkey. These coins, from c550 BC, were small gold pieces stamped with a lion and a bull. King Pheidon of Argos minted silver coins stamped with a turtle, and some claim that he produced his coins before Croesus, but the dates when Pheidon lived are disputed.

# GRAPHIC HISTORY
### AD 79 volcanic disaster in facts and figures

# WHAT HAPPENED WHEN VESUVIUS BLEW ITS TOP?

**1.8**
Even before the first deadly pyroclastic flow struck Pompeii, as much as **1.8 metres of ash** had settled on the ground in some areas.

## VESUVIUS

The volcano's eruption in AD 79 plunged the towns of **Pompeii and Herculaneum** into darkness, before smothering them with pyroclastic flows – fast-moving tides of superheated ash, smoke, gas and rock.

**Forum**
The centre of business, religion and politics in the city encompassed offices, temples, baths, a market place and the basilica, which served as a court.

**House of the Vettii**
One of the most luxurious villas to be discovered, this house boasted elaborate frescoes and a garden studded with bronze and marble statues.

## POMPEII

Before Vesuvius erupted, **Pompeii was in its heyday**. The town was the stomping ground of the well-to-do – it's thought even Emperor Nero had a pad nearby.

**House of the Faun**
This 3,000m² villa owned by wealthy aristocrats covered a whole block. It's named for a bronze statuette found in the atrium, and boasts fine mosaics.

**1/3**
The proportion of slaves in the city's population

**Gladiator barracks**
Enslaved fighters trained for battle in the barracks set behind one of the smaller theatres.

## HOW THE DISASTER UNFOLDED

| 24 AUGUST | | | | | 25 AUGUST | | | | | | 26 AUGUST |
|---|---|---|---|---|---|---|---|---|---|---|---|

12am 2am 4am 6am 8am 10am 12pm 2pm 4pm 6pm 8pm 10pm 12am 2am 4am 6am 8am 10am 12pm 2pm 4pm 6pm 8pm 10pm 12am

Vesuvius rumbles into life with a series of small gas and ash emissions.

The volcano erupts, sending a cloud of ash and smoke over 20km into the sky. The cloud stretches south, plunging Pompeii into darkness.

Quakes recur all afternoon, and buildings collapse. Many flee to the sea, but floating volcanic debris blocks the port.

According to Pliny the Younger's eyewitness account, the sea level falls, indicating an imminent tsunami.

The cloud of ash and smoke towers 25km above the volcano, lit by electrical storms. The cloud reaches Misenum, from where Pliny the Younger is watching.

Mudflows carrying scalding volcanic material tear towards Herculaneum, destroying the town.

The cloud reaches 30km high and collapses in on itself, sending a superheated pyroclastic flow towards Herculaneum, killing everyone.

A second pyroclastic surge hits Herculaneum.

Several massive pyroclastic flows obliterate Pompeii. The last surge sweeps as far as Stabiae.

The worst has passed, but Vesuvius rumbles on for days, generating thunderstorms and mudslides. By the time the eruption is finished, the summit of Vesuvius is 200m lower.

**1,000**
At the time of the cataclysm that engulfed Pompeii, **Vesuvius had not produced a significant eruption** for 1,000 years – so the residents didn't realise the danger.

**30**
At its tallest, **the column of ash, rock and smoke** may have risen 30km – three times the height at which modern commercial planes fly.

**2,000**
About 2,000 people died at **Pompeii**, out of a population of some 12,000-15,000. The survivors most likely fled as the eruption began.

**700**
The pyroclastic flow could have **reached speeds of up to 700kph**. If so, it would have hit Pompeii in less than a minute.

**6**
The number of public *thermae* (baths) found in Pompeii

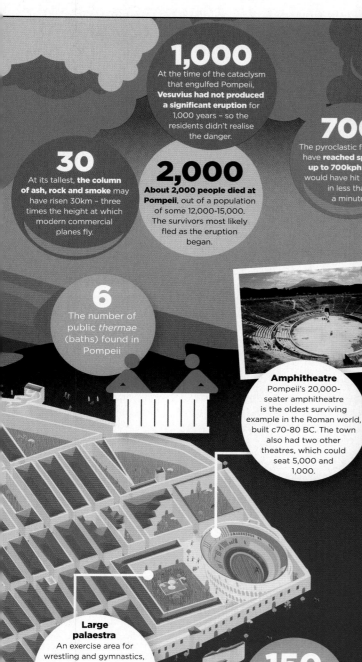

**Amphitheatre**
Pompeii's 20,000-seater amphitheatre is the oldest surviving example in the Roman world, built c70-80 BC. The town also had two other theatres, which could seat 5,000 and 1,000.

**Large palaestra**
An exercise area for wrestling and gymnastics, with a swimming pool in the centre, this space may have doubled as a gathering place for spectators heading to the amphitheatre.

**150**
The number of bars believed to have flourished in pre-eruption Pompeii

# WHERE IT HAPPENED

NAPLES

VESUVIUS

HERCULANEUM

MISENUM

POMPEII

BAY OF NAPLES

VOLCANIC CLOUD

STABIAE

The only surviving eyewitness account of the catastrophe is by Roman official **Pliny the Younger** who saw the eruption from Misenum, 35km away.

## STATISTICS

**POMPEII**

**Size:** 660,000m²
**Population:** 12,000-15,000
**Distance from Vesuvius:** 10km
**Depth of ash:** up to 5m

**HERCULANEUM**

**Size:** 165,000m²
**Population:** 4,000-5,000
**Distance from Vesuvius:** 6km
**Depth of ash:** up to 20m

**500°C** Temperature of the pyroclastic flows that struck Herculaneum

**300°C** Temperature of the pyroclastic flows that struck Pompeii

**212°C** Temperature at which leather autoignites

**150°C** Temperature at which wood chars

**44°C** Temperature at which skin begins to burn

# SET IN STONE

Anyone who has been to Pompeii will recall the striking models of Vesuvius's victims. These casts were made by pouring plaster into the cavities left in the volcanic layers once the engulfed dead had decomposed. Some of the models are remarkably detailed, and the agony of the victims as they were blanketed by bone-scorchingly hot ash is often painfully clear to see.

## TIMELINE OF DISCOVERY

Though the eruption blotted out all life in the two towns, the hot ash preserved the settlements phenomenally well, as 18th-century archaeologists discovered to their delight

**1709-10**
A theatre is discovered at Herculaneum. Many statues and other artefacts are removed and later sold across Europe.

**1738**
Excavation begins at Herculaneum by order of the King of Naples.

**1748**
Official excavation begins at Pompeii. The name of the town is still unknown.

**1763**
Pompeii is definitively identified after the discovery of an inscription that includes the name of the town. By 1780, excavation at Herculaneum is halted, with resources redirected to the Pompeii site.

**1900s**
Excavation continues sporadically at both sites, and plaster casts of the victims begin to be made (see Set in Stone, above).

**1924-61**
Major excavations are undertaken. In 1962, the works are restricted to a few discrete areas in an attempt to prevent further damage and decay.

**1981-98**
Some 300 bodies are discovered at the beach near Herculaneum.

# Was King Herod really so bad?

No ancient monarch was ever particularly 'good', but Herod I of Judea (reigned 37-4 BC) perhaps has a worse reputation than any other. Of Arab ethnicity, Herod owed his position in Judea to the backing of Romans, who had helped bring him to power. Determined to ape Rome, Herod developed a series of ambitious building projects, including the establishment of Caesarea as the main harbour and the rebuilding of the Second Temple in Jerusalem. His non-Jewish heritage did not sit well with the religious elite of Judea, though, and some political factions saw him as little more than a puppet of Rome.

The later years of Herod's reign were marked by illness and paranoia, leading him to murder one of his wives and two of his sons. His chief claim to infamy, however, was the 'Massacre of the Innocents' – the infanticide designed to ensure the death of the prophesied newborn 'King of the Jews' – recorded in the Gospel of Matthew. This horrific event was not mentioned in any of the other gospels, nor by any contemporary Jewish source, and modern historians have cast doubt on whether it actually happened. Overall, then, though a despot and tyrant, Herod was no worse than any other ruler of the period.

**Herod reputedly ordered the slaughter of Bethlehem's babies**

ALAMY X2, GETTY X5, THINKSTOCK X1

# WHO WERE THE HUNS?

**ENEMY AT THE GATES**
The warlike Huns, led by the infamous Attila, threatened the security of the city of Rome in the fifth century AD

The short answer is: we don't really know. Originating from somewhere in Central Asia, the people known as Huns first appeared on the borders of the Roman Empire in the fourth century AD. The Romans found them particularly terrifying because, unlike other so-called barbarians, their customs, religion, lifestyle and language seemed incomprehensible. From the Romans' perspective, the aggressive Huns had no clear targets (land, for example), so successive emperors found it easiest to simply pay them off with gold. A continual threat to Roman security, the Huns were seen as the antithesis of Mediterranean-style civilisation and, as a consequence, were frequently portrayed in overtly negative, almost 'demonic' terms. Sadly, no objective description of them survives and, as they failed to record their own experiences in any meaningful way, our understanding of who they were and what they wanted from Rome is deeply flawed.

**55** The number, in thousands, of miles of paved roads built by the Romans across the Empire – enough to circle the world seven times.

# WHY DID THE ROMANS BUILD STRAIGHT ROADS?

While some Roman roads might have bends or corners, the vast majority are distinctively straight as they march for mile after mile across Britain and Europe. Unlike modern roads, the *via munita* were not intended for the use of ordinary people. Only army units, government officials and those with a special pass were allowed to use them. When moving armies, or officials to deal with emergencies, speed was paramount. Everyone else had to make do with using local dirt tracks.

You would think certain natural features – steep hills and valleys – of the landscape could affect the straightness of the *via munita*. Not so, Roman roads went straight up the most precipitous of slopes without winding back and forth in hairpin bends like modern roads. This is because a marching man on foot can go straight up a steep hill and then rest to recover before moving on much quicker than if he wound around a gently rising slope. Army supplies were carried on mules who could likewise go up a steep slope without much trouble.

**STRAIGHT AS A RULER**
The strength of Roman roads means that many still exist today, while others became the foundations of other roads

# WHO WAS THE LAST PHARAOH OF EGYPT?

The last ruler of Egypt before it was successfully invaded by the Roman Empire was Cleopatra VII, who died in 30 BC. However, the Roman ruler Augustus chose to lead Egypt independently of Rome, using the title of pharaoh in order to keep the vast income of the Egyptian state in his hands. Although Egypt had the same ruler as the Roman Empire, it remained a separate state. The last Roman Emperor to have called himself pharaoh and to have ruled Egypt separately from Rome was Decius (AD 249-251).

## WHAT DOES 'SPQR' MEAN?

◉ SPQR, which was displayed on most Roman inscriptions and monuments, and can now be seen emblazoned across military standards in every Hollywood epic, stands for the Latin phrase *Senatus Populusque Romanus*. It means 'the Senate and people of Rome' – a reminder that Rome was, supposedly, a Republic where the people had the last word. Even after the Republic effectively died in the late first century BC and was replaced by the Roman Empire, SPQR continued to be used in order to sustain the image that Rome was a monarch-free state.

# How many pyramid tombs are there in Egypt?

**TIP OF THE ICEBERG**
Saqqara is famous, but Egypt has many more pyramids

◉ Although most tourists concentrate on the huge pyramids at Giza and Saqqara, there are many other pyramids in Egypt. All of them have four triangular sides sloping up from a square base. The shape symbolised the rays of the Sun reaching down to Earth, with the polished sides reflecting the light. The shape also mimicked the primordial mound that, in Egyptian religion, had been the first part of the Earth to emerge from the ancient waters. Every pyramid was built on the west bank of the Nile. This put them close to the setting Sun and so to the mythological realm of the dead.

Archaeologists have identified a total of 118 pyramid tombs in Egypt. Most of these are relatively small and some of the poorly built ones have collapsed into piles of rubble. As recently as 2008, the ruins of a pyramid emerged from sand dunes near Saqqara, so it's thought that other undiscovered pyramids may exist.

## DID YOU KNOW?

**SICK NOTE**
The idea that a vomitorium was a room where Romans threw up, making space for more food, is a myth. The vomitorium was instead a passageway in a theatre, providing audiences with a rapid exit – allowing them to 'spew forth' onto the streets.

# Why did the Romans take so many baths?

◉ The Roman baths were similar to 'Turkish' baths or saunas: a series of progressively hotter rooms intermixed with warm and cold immersion baths. Bathing was a major activity in the Roman world. This wasn't because of any desire to be clean – most Roman bathhouses were loud, unhealthy places where all social classes who could afford the entrance ticket rubbed up against one another (quite literally) – but because they represented the best place to exercise, socialise and do business. Rome had no equivalent of pubs, clubs or gyms, so most establishments provided not only baths but also exercise halls, libraries (to exercise the mind), barbers, gaming rooms and areas to eat and drink. For modesty's sake, men and women had segregated baths or bathed at different times. Visits to the urban baths, once the morning work was done, took up the better part of the day. Bathing and the provision of public baths fell out of fashion in post-Roman Europe. The Christian society thought bathing was a decadent luxury that weakened an individual's body discipline and could lead to lascivious thoughts and 'unholy' activities.

## HOW DEMOCRATIC WAS ANCIENT ATHENS?

◉ Not very. Although celebrated as the birthplace of democracy, not everyone in fifth-century-BC Athens had the right to vote. Of the 250,000 people living there, less than an eighth were permitted to vote. Women, slaves or non-Athenians (traders, visitors or refugees) were denied such rights.

# HOW DID THEY DO THAT?
# GREAT WALL OF CHINA

## The bulwarks that took two millennia to build

◎ There are several misconceptions about the Great Wall of China, which snakes its way through the Chinese countryside. It is not a single wall, but a series of fortifications (some of which run parallel to each other), and there is no truth to the legend that the Great Wall can be seen from space. Yet it is undoubtedly one of the most impressive pieces of architecture and engineering in history – a project that was ongoing for 2,000 years.

## THE FIRST EMPEROR

Wall fortifications were first built during the seventh century BC, but when Qin Shi Huang conquered the individual Chinese kingdoms and united China – becoming the first Emperor in 221 BC – he ordered that the sections of wall be joined into one great defence.

**EMPIRE BUILDER**
Qin also expanded China's road system and built the Terracotta Army

## A LEGENDARY PLACE
Dozens of legends surround the Great Wall. One of the most enduring is the myth of Meng Jiangnu, the wife of one of the builders who died. According to the story, when she learned of his death, she cried so hard that it caused a section of the wall to collapse.

## STILL STRONG
While some sections of the wall are in poor condition, or have been destroyed, the best preserved example of the Great Wall dates from the Ming dynasty – and runs for some 5,500 miles.

## BUILDING THE WALL

The first walls were constructed to protect individual kingdoms in China from warring neighbours. The most common construction method in the seventh century BC was 'rammed earth' – packing soil tightly into a natural bulwark. Over the centuries, the Qin wall was added to by several dynasties. During the Ming dynasty (1368-1644), fears of a Mongol invasion led to extensive rebuilding using state-of-the-art techniques.

**Qin dynasty**
If rock from nearby mountains couldn't be collected, earth and small stones were compacted to build a natural wall.

**Han, Jin, Sui dynasties**
Until the seventh century AD, various methods were adopted, including using a wooden frame to hold together a mixture of water and gravel.

**Ming dynasty**
Bricks – which were stronger so could bear more weight – were increasingly used to build and repair sections of wall quickly.

6m | 5m

6-10m

**Some of the towers are approximately 500 metres apart**

## SNAKING ALONG
The wall utilised the natural terrain, from hills to rivers, to improve defences

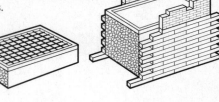

ILLUSTRATION: SOL 90, ALAMY X1, SHEU-XUEI HO X2

**CHINA**

Beijing · Shanghai
Badaling

**Qin Dynasty**
**221-206 BC**

**Ming Dynasty**
**1368-1644**

**THE TOTAL LENGTH OF THE GREAT WALL: 13,171 miles**
But, if you added up all the branches built throughout the Great Wall's history, then its total length is believed to be long enough to almost circle the planet twice.

## WALK THE WALL
The most popular section for tourists is Badaling – built in the Ming dynasty

## THE BATTLEMENTS
In the Ming dynasty, detachments of soldiers were stationed in each tower, either to stand on watch for foreign invasion or to protect the traders passing through the wall on their way to the Silk Road to Europe.

## SOLID FOUNDATIONS
It is impossible to know how many millions of construction workers were used over the millennia to build the wall. Those who died – which could number in the hundreds of thousands – were buried in the foundations of the wall.

## REACHING HIGH
To build the watch towers, bamboo was used as scaffolding. It is so strong that it is still used in China today.

## LIGHT THE BEACONS
During the Ming dynasty, watch towers were developed to warn of a Mongol invasion. A column of smoke was sent up in daytime to let the next watch tower know that an enemy army was approaching. At night, huge bonfires were built.

**EEL APPEAL**
For the first time, the popularity of jellied eels is on the rise outside of London's East End

# WHY DID JELLIED EELS GO OUT OF FASHION?

The answer to this mystery lies with the eels themselves. The European eel (*Anguilla anguilla*) can survive in brackish and poorly oxygenated waters, a quality that made it a particularly common fish along the Thames Estuary downstream of London, as well as in the marshes and swamps of Essex. Eels were caught in these areas in vast numbers, then taken up the Thames to Billingsgate Fish Market which, by the mid-19th century, was the largest fish market in the world. While more expensive fish went to the homes of the rich, the cheap eels were taken by cart to the East End of London.

There the eels provided an inexpensive source of protein at a time when meat was generally expensive. The eels were cut into chunks (a process known as shucking), then boiled in water and vinegar. This released collagen-rich proteins into the water-vinegar mix so that when the mix was poured into a bowl and allowed to cool it solidified into a jelly.

By the 1820s, it was customary to serve jellied eels with pie and mash, giving rise to the famous eel, pie and mash shops of the East End. By the mid-20th century, however, increasing pollution in the Thames and the draining of most of the Essex marshland brought an end to the mass supply of cheap eels. Although eels continued to be brought into London from further afield, prices soared. By the 1950s, jellied eel was a delicacy rather than a staple food, although a resurgence in their popularity has occurred of late.

# Which is the **oldest pub** in England?

The right answer to this question rather depends on what criteria you use. For instance, does it mean the oldest building or the longest continuous use as a pub? Several establishments lay claim to the title, based on the different options. The Old Ferryboat at St Ives in Cambridgeshire appears in the Domesday Book and claims to date back to AD 560, though the current building is far newer.

Ye Olde Fighting Cocks at St Albans has been operating from the current building since 1485, while Ye Olde Trip to Jerusalem, in Nottingham, claims to have been founded in 1189 to cater to men setting out on Crusade, although the current building is only about 350 years old.

The Bingley Arms in Bardsey, West Yorkshire, claims that a pub mentioned in parish records of AD 953 refer to itself, but this is far from clear and the current building is just four centuries old.

Investigations at the Eagle & Child at Stow-on-the-Wold in Gloucestershire have proved that some of the timbers used in its construction are more than 1,000 years old, but the building has not always been a pub.

Ye Olde Man and Scythe in Bolton has a cellar that dates back to before 1251, though the building above it was rebuilt in 1636.

**BOTTOMS UP**
**Inns and taverns – and the beer they serve – have long been an important part of British society**

## WHY DID WE BOYCOTT SUGAR IN THE 1700s?

**Europe had a sweet tooth in the 18th century. Cane sugar, cakes, patisseries and icing were the treats du jour. But the sugar crop was harvested by enslaved Africans. Every spoonful helped the slave trade to continue, so abolitionists called on everyone to boycott slave-grown sweet stuff. Soon, home-grown sugar became available.**

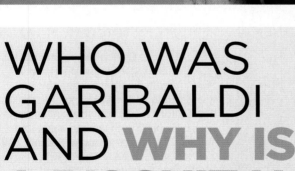

**45** **The amount, in kilos, of scurvy-stopping sauerkraut with lime juice taken on Captain Cook's 1768-71 circumnavigation.**

# WHO WAS GARIBALDI AND **WHY IS A BISCUIT NAMED AFTER HIM**?

**Giuseppe Garibaldi was a 19th-century Italian guerrilla fighter and revolutionary who led rebellions against Austrian control of the Italian peninsula. The Victorians had a soft spot for rebels – unless they were rebelling against British rule! – particularly Italians.**

**Garibaldi first became popular in Britain for leading the heroic-but-doomed defence of Rome against the Austrians. He earned a lot of British sympathy, especially as his wife was killed in the fighting. During his time spent in Britain, he became a celebrity, with Victorian homes displaying prints and busts of him. With Garibaldi becoming a well-known name, a new biscuit, first made in 1861, was named in his honour. The biccie consists of two soft (by Victorian standards) rectangular slabs of biscuits, sandwiching a bed of currants.**

# Did Britain ever have any form of **prohibition**?

The first of many societies advocating temperance, opposing drunkenness and excessive consumption of spirits, was established in the 1830s. As the movement grew, many began to encourage total abstinence as part of the 19th-century zeal for social and moral reform.

The movement gave rise to magazines, hotels, cautionary art and literature, marches and public lectures, as well as the promotion of alternatives, such as milk and tea. The politically minded argued that the working classes, who were seeking the vote, would gain respectability by embracing sobriety.

Despite the apparent success of such moral persuasion, attempts to set this in law – such as the 1854 Sale of Beer Act that limited Sunday opening hours – led to widespread rioting. Calls for prohibition were met with open hostility well into the 20th century.

**BATTLE OF THE BOTTLE**
Victorian temperance cartoons showed how alcohol fuelled murderous rages

## DID THE ITALIANS **INVENT SPAGHETTI**?

Noodles were being made in China centuries before they first appeared in Italy around 1300. It is often said that Marco Polo brought the recipe for noodles to Italy after his journeys through China, and so most people believe that the Italians did not invent spaghetti.

The spaghetti that most people eat today, however, is quite different from the noodles of yesteryear. Earlier noodles were made by mixing flour with eggs, the resulting mixture being cut to shape and laid out in the sun to dry. Modern pasta has no eggs and is dried in special chambers where cool air is circulated around the pasta to ensure it dries evenly to avoid cracking or warping. This type of spaghetti was very definitely invented by the Italians. In fact, it was the creation of one Italian in particular: Nicola de Cecco.

De Cecco ran a flour mill at Fara San Martino in Abruzzo. He was dissatisfied with the sun-drying of pasta as it gave unreliable results, and the pasta often warped, making it difficult to package for transport. In 1886, he developed his method of drying pasta in cool, dry conditions and founded the De Cecco company. He later adopted a logo of a young country woman carrying a sheaf of wheat and went into mass production. The company is still operating in Fara San Martino; a second factory was built in the nearby town of Pescara in the 1950s.

So although noodles and pasta may not have originated in Italy, we certainly do have an Italian to thank for the modern form of pasta enjoyed today right around the world.

**8,200** The number of sheep eaten by the Tudor court in an average year

## WHAT WAS **NEGUS**?

Colonel Francis Negus, an English military officer and politician, is credited with inventing this hot, spiced drink, which was popular in the early 18th century. Made from fortified wine (sherry or port) with lemons, sugar and nutmeg, negus was a must at Regency balls and was mentioned in *Vanity Fair*, *Wuthering Heights*, *Jane Eyre* and many of Dickens' novels. By mid-Victorian times, it had fallen out of fashion; in 1861, Mrs Beeton had recommended it for children's parties, suggesting one pint of wine per nine or ten kids.

**COOKING THE BOOKS**
By the Victorian era, Negus was considered a children's drink, as Mrs Beeton's recipe confirms

## HOW DOES CIDER LINK NORMANDY AND SOMERSET?

Cider making is an ancient art. When the Romans arrived in Britain, they recorded that the local Celts fermented crab-apple juice into a harsh, alcoholic drink. It is thought that when the Normans invaded England in 1066, they brought new varieties of special cider apples with them. However, the traditions and skills of cider making in both locations seem to have then developed separately.

In short, the two regions share a drink not so much through direct cultural links, but because both have soils and climates that are suited to the cultivation of fruit trees.

**WHAT WILL YOU HAVE?**
Full English fry ups have grown to include baked beans, mushrooms and anything else you desire

# WHY IS A FRY-UP BREAKFAST CALLED A 'FULL ENGLISH'?

It is a traditional favourite, truckers' saviour and miracle hangover cure. The 'full English' breakfast – consisting of sausages, bacon, eggs, tomatoes, toast and some black pudding if you're so inclined – is a firmly established national dish. Yet, while fried food has been eaten for centuries, the meal wasn't adopted as 'English' until the 20th century.

Its name grew as the meal was increasingly seen as an alternative to decidedly healthier 'Continental' breakfasts of pastries and fruit juices offered to tourists in Britain. But the English aren't the only ones claiming the fry-up. The 'full Scottish' includes potato scones, while the 'full Welsh' comes with laverbread and the 'Ulster fry' with soda bread. Or there's the Canadian 'Lumberjack Breakfast', complete with pancakes.

# When did the English fall **in love with tea**?

Sitting down with a nice cup of tea is as quintessentially English as it gets, but that wasn't always the case. The English love affair with tea goes back only to the latter half of the 17th century, with the arrival of the Portuguese Princess Catherine of Braganza, soon to be queen of Charles II, in 1662. Although the drink had already reached England – two years earlier the diarist Samuel Pepys had noted sampling "a Cup of Tee (a China drink)" for the first time – Catherine was dismayed to find that the favourite beverage of her native court was not popular in her new home. She quickly introduced tea-drinking as a fashionable pursuit in aristocratic circles.

In the decades that followed, the growing popular enthusiasm for tea provoked great debate. Some believed that, along with the other new 'hot liquors' coffee and hot chocolate, it could bring on nervous disorders and even premature death. In 1822, the reformer William Cobbett claimed that tea-drinking made men effeminate and turned women to a life of debauchery – his ingenious solution was to brew "wholesome beer" instead.

However, thanks to the Temperance Movement's promotion of tea as a safer alternative to alcohol for the working classes, as well as the development of fashionable afternoon tea-parties among the well-to-do, by the mid-19th-century tea had been established as England's national drink.

**FANCY A CUPPA?**
The British Empire is described as being "built on tea"

# GRAPHIC HISTORY
## A visual guide to events from the past

# HOW LONG DID RATIONING LAST AFTER WORLD WAR II?

## WHAT WAS RATIONED?

**PETROL**
Rationed for 11 years – 1939–1950

**SOAP**
Rationed for 8 years – 1942–1950

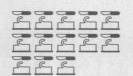

**BUTTER**
Rationed for 13 years – 1940–1953

Between 1941 and 1944, over **100 million tins** of SPAM were shipped to Europe from the US. In the UK, it was the only meat **never controlled** by rationing.

## THE BASIC FOOD RATION PER PERSON PER WEEK IN 1942

On top of these rationed items, a person could boost their diet with as many **vegetables** as they could get. They weren't rationed, but limited supply led to a **grow-your-own movement** that swept the country.

Although not deemed nutritional, tea was considered important for its **psychological benefits** – it had the comfort factor. When rationed, a person could have 2oz a week. Manual labourers had an **extra allowance**.

**1 egg**

MARGARINE

**4oz special margarine**
Boosted with vitamins

**2-4oz cheese**

## THE BIGGER PICTURE

After VE day, on 8 May 1945, there was a drop in food supply, rather than an increase so, for a time, **rationing became more severe**. As the Allies took responsibility for **feeding war-torn countries** around the world, Britain also wanted to avoid **escalating prices** that may have come with a sudden availability of food. A gradual lift on rationing was essential.

Before the war, in 1939, more than 60% of **Britain's food was imported**.

By the end of 1940, U-boats had sunk **728,000 tons of food** destined for the British Isles.

728,000

INFOGRAPHIC: TIDY DESIGNS

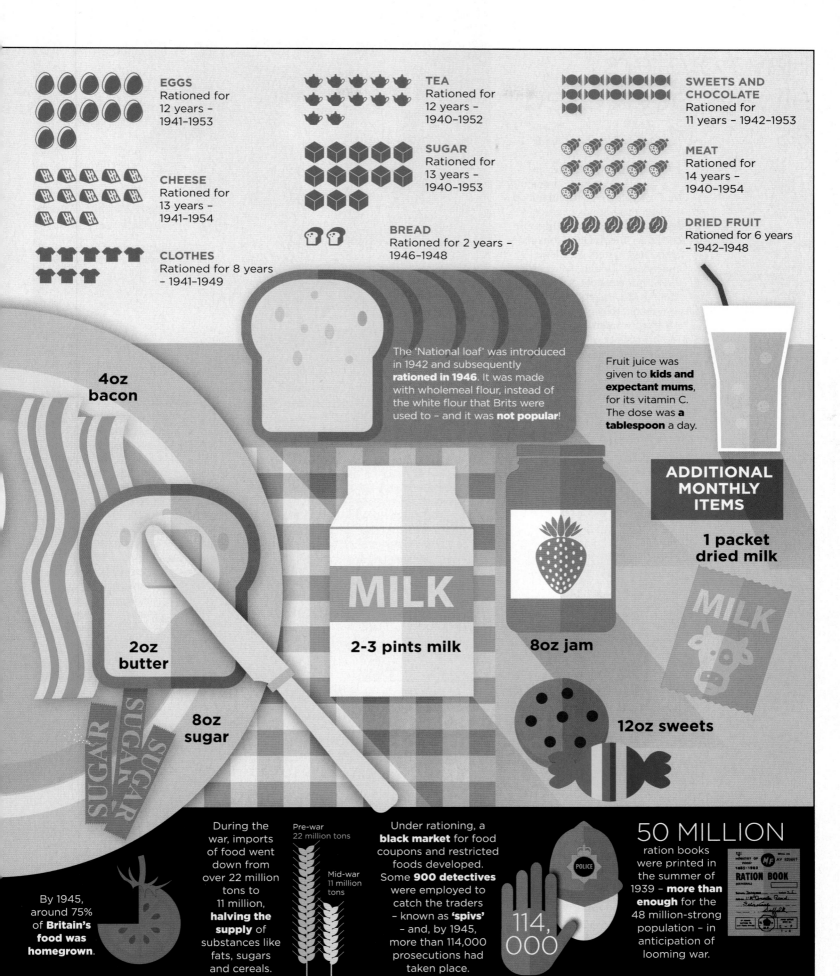

**EGGS**
Rationed for 12 years – 1941–1953

**CHEESE**
Rationed for 13 years – 1941–1954

**CLOTHES**
Rationed for 8 years – 1941–1949

**TEA**
Rationed for 12 years – 1940–1952

**SUGAR**
Rationed for 13 years – 1940–1953

**BREAD**
Rationed for 2 years – 1946–1948

**SWEETS AND CHOCOLATE**
Rationed for 11 years – 1942–1953

**MEAT**
Rationed for 14 years – 1940–1954

**DRIED FRUIT**
Rationed for 6 years – 1942–1948

The 'National loaf' was introduced in 1942 and subsequently **rationed in 1946**. It was made with wholemeal flour, instead of the white flour that Brits were used to – and it was **not popular**!

Fruit juice was given to **kids and expectant mums**, for its vitamin C. The dose was **a tablespoon** a day.

**4oz bacon**

**2oz butter**

**8oz sugar**

**2-3 pints milk**

**8oz jam**

**12oz sweets**

**ADDITIONAL MONTHLY ITEMS**

**1 packet dried milk**

By 1945, around 75% of **Britain's food was homegrown**.

During the war, imports of food went down from over 22 million tons to 11 million, **halving the supply** of substances like fats, sugars and cereals.

Pre-war 22 million tons

Mid-war 11 million tons

Under rationing, a **black market** for food coupons and restricted foods developed. Some **900 detectives** were employed to catch the traders – known as **'spivs'** – and, by 1945, more than 114,000 prosecutions had taken place.

114,000

POLICE

**50 MILLION** ration books were printed in the summer of 1939 – **more than enough** for the 48 million-strong population – in anticipation of looming war.

RATION BOOK

# Have oysters always been used as *aphrodisiacs*?

In its quest for pleasure and procreation, humanity has linked particular foods to lust for thousands of years – and the oyster is one of the most enduring. The Ancient Romans associated oysters with lewd practices, although the reasons aren't immediately clear. The Roman satirical poet Juvenal wrote that they were devoured by loose women. In the 1700s, notorious lothario Casanova seduced women with oysters and champagne, as "a spur to spirit and to love", and their reputation remains potent to this day. Other supposed aphrodisiacs have (thankfully) waned over time, including offal, sparrow brains and raw onion.

**BROTHER BUBBLES**
Dom Pérignon is credited with creating champagne – but in fact he worked hard to keep his wine still

## WHO INVENTED CHAMPAGNE?

On 4 August 1693, a Benedictine monk called Dom Pierre Pérignon shouted excitedly for his monastic brothers. "Come quickly! I am drinking the stars!" he exclaimed, having at last cracked the secret to producing sparkling champagne.

Or so the story goes. Alas, this charming anecdote is a 19th-century myth. In fact, Dom Pérignon worked tirelessly to eradicate bubbles in the wine of his region, Champagne. When bottled wine cooled before all of the sugar had been converted into alcohol, fermentation halted. Then, when bottles warmed up again in the summer, dormant yeasts became active, producing carbon dioxide and effervescence. The build-up of pressure made many bottles of poor-quality French glass explode in the cellar – hence the contents were known as the 'devil's wine'.

In fact, there's evidence that the method for encouraging secondary fermentation to produce sparkling wine was first described in England in 1662. English glass was tougher than French and used airtight corks, so very fizzy wine could be enjoyed as a thrilling novelty.

By the early 18th century, the French aristocracy had acquired the taste, and marques such as Veuve Clicquot, Krug and Bollinger were later launched. The champagne called Dom Pérignon was first produced in 1921 – and now the 'devil's wine' is the most famous in the world!

### DID YOU KNOW?

**EATING THEIR WORDS**
In 1894, there were reports in English culinary journal *The Table* that an Australian confectioner had "hit upon the brilliant idea" of an edible newspaper, with the affairs of the day printed in liquid chocolate onto a thin paste of dough.

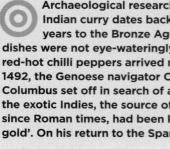

## WHAT DOES CHRISTOPHER COLUMBUS HAVE TO DO WITH INDIAN CURRY?

Archaeological research proves that Indian curry dates back thousands of years to the Bronze Age. However, such dishes were not eye-wateringly spicy; indeed, red-hot chilli peppers arrived much later. In 1492, the Genoese navigator Christopher Columbus set off in search of a short route to the exotic Indies, the source of pepper, which, since Roman times, had been known as 'black gold'. On his return to the Spanish court, he presented plants that he claimed were pepper, but which were called *aji* or *chilli* by the native Americans. Soon, European merchants – particularly Portuguese traders – began spreading mislabelled 'chilli peppers' throughout Eurasia, where they were quickly adopted into local cuisine. In fact, by the time the British arrived in India, they were convinced the fiery chilli pepper was native to the subcontinent.

## IS THE BAKEWELL TART FROM BAKEWELL?

Up to a point. The Bakewell tart that's sold today, as pictured below, seems to have originated in the early 20th century and is only distantly related to the Bakewell pudding, which *did* originate in the Derbyshire town.

The pudding consists of a flaky pastry shell lined with a thick layer of jam and filled with egg custard mixed with ground almonds to make a hot dessert. It was created by Mrs Greaves, landlady of the town's White Horse Inn, at some point in the late 18th or early 19th centuries. Three different shops now sell puddings, each one of which claims to use the original, highly secret recipe.

## WHERE DID BANOFFEE PIE COME FROM?

Inspired by schoolboy experiments that boiled condensed milk inside the can to create toffee, it took chef Ian Dowding and owner Nigel Mackenzie, of the Hungry Monk restaurant in Jevington, East Sussex, two years to perfect their new gut-busting dessert recipe. After numerous abortive attempts with various 'wrong' fruits, including apples and mandarins, the pie was introduced to pudding lovers in 1972. However, they never bothered to copyright the name – a lesson for us all...

## WHAT FAST FOOD WAS EATEN IN VICTORIAN BRITAIN?

Quickly grabbing cheap food from market stalls and street-barrows had long been a staple of the working-class diet, but by the 19th century, customers were being treated to an array of new flavours. Thanks to changing tastes, taxes and competition from larger shops, by the 1850s vendors of hot pies, eels and roast apples were being gradually replaced by coffee stalls and ice-cream barrows. Hot baked potatoes and pineapple slices also became more popular, although traditional foods didn't disappear altogether. In 1870, an American reporter described the wares on sale at a London market: "ham sandwiches, at a penny apiece, and boiled potatoes, with sheeps' trotters, oysters, fried fish, oranges, apples, plums, and, in fact, every kind of fruit and vegetable were for sale" – as well as "a very suspicious veal".

## HAVE THE BRITISH ALWAYS BEEN HEAVY DRINKERS?

The creation and consumption of alcohol existed in most early agricultural societies, with Britain being no exception. Cereal-based residues, attributed to the brewing of beer, have been found on pottery dating to the third millennium BC. By the first century AD, many Mediterranean writers were commenting on the love that the people of northern Europe had for "fermented grain", which was (allegedly) drunk to excess. Whereas Greek and Roman societies drank wine with food – a practice still seen in countries like France and Italy – northern European culture was built more firmly around the communal feast where the grain, not the grape, featured. Barley-based 'Celtic beer' was renowned throughout the Roman Empire, while first-century British kings proudly displayed ears of barley on their coinage as signifiers of wealth.

The importance of alcohol had quite an effect on the Romans in Britannia. A letter surviving from Vindolanda (a fort close to Hadrian's Wall) reads, "My fellow soldiers have no beer.

**BOTTOMS UP!**
While the Romans were sipping wine, the Britons enjoyed the "fermented grain"

Please order some to be sent." With the coming of the warrior-based Germanic societies that dominated Britain in the post-Roman period, the heroic levels of alcohol use already in existence in the islands were added to, increasing the belief that the phenomenon of drunkenness was a curiously British trait.

# HOW DID THEY DO THAT?
# AL KHAZNEH

## Petra's most elaborate and beautiful ruin

Hidden among the canyons and desert dunes of Jordan is Petra, an ancient city carved by the Nabataean people from the very cliffs of sandstone. The centrepiece of the 'rose red city' is the temple of Al Khazneh...

## WORLD WONDER
Petra is Jordan's most visited tourist attraction and one of the world's architectural wonders. In 1985, Petra was made a UNESCO World Heritage Site.

## THE ROAD TO AL KHAZNEH
The main way to reach Al Khazneh is the Siq, a narrow path running though a crack in the canyon and loomed over by the towering cliff walls. The path then opens up dramatically to reveal Al Khazneh.

## THE ROSE CITY
The sandstone that forms the cliffs at Petra has a high iron content, giving the rock its iconic reddish-pink hue. The colour of the rock has led some to call Petra the 'Rose City'.

## LOWER TOMBS
In 2003, archaeologists discovered four burial chambers approximately six metres below the surface. They contained human bones and hooks for hanging offerings of incense.

## CARVING AL KHAZNEH
The creation of Al Khazneh, thought to have been between first century BC and first century AD, was no easy feat. Before work began on the 12-storey structure, the builders had to scale the cliff. What makes the accomplishment more extraordinary is that Al Khazneh was carved from a single rock...

### 1. FLATTENING THE CLIFF FACE
Starting 40 metres up the cliff, the builders tunnelled straight along the rock face to create a platform to stand on. Then using pick axes, they gradually worked downwards, making a smooth surface.

### 2. CARVING THE FACADE
The facade was then carved top down. There was no margin for error as the builders had to ensure that the upper section was not too heavy for the bottom (not yet carved) causing it to collapse.

### 3. INSIDE THE STRUCTURE
Tunnels were then carved deep into the cliff, again from the top down, to create the entrance and inner chambers. Al Khazneh has only a few chambers behind the impressive facade.

### 4. REMOVING THE WASTE
Unwanted rock was transported to nearby sites at Petra so it could be used to build other structures. Emptying the interior would have required the moving of thousands of cubic metres of rock.

ILLUSTRATION: SOL 90, THINKSTOCK X2

## HIDDEN TREASURE

Near the top of Al Khazneh is a large stone urn, the carvings on which are badly damaged and chipped. This wasn't due to erosion, however, but gunshots. Bedouins, believing it to be full of treasure hidden by bandits, would shoot at the urn in the hope it would shatter and the treasure would rain down.

The first sight of Al Khazneh from the approach along the Siq gorge

## WHO BUILT PETRA?

The columned architecture, imposing sculptures and intricate carvings initially fooled archaeologists into thinking Al Khazneh had been built by the Ancient Greeks. However, the real builders were the Nabataeans, a nomadic tribe running enormous camel caravans across the trade routes of the Arabian Desert on to the Mediterranean.

## INSIDE THE TEMPLE

There is not much to see beyond the breathtaking entrance as there are only a few rooms. It is thought Al Khazneh was built to be a crypt or a temple.

**3. MAIN CHAMBER**

**4. TOMBS**

**1. HALL**

**2. SIDE CHAMBERS**

## THE CARVINGS

Many carvings adorn the facade of Al Khazneh, mostly representing the afterlife. Flanking the entrance are two men on horseback – the twins Castor and Pollux who guided the souls of fallen heroes.

## WHAT IS THE SIGNIFICANCE OF THE **BULLDOG**?

⊙ There are several breeds of bulldog today, including the small French, the powerful American and the wrinkled British, but the original breed that earned notoriety is now extinct. The Old English Bulldog possessed a muscular, stocky body and a vice-like jaw that clamped shut with tremendous force, making it well-suited to the violent sport of bullbaiting. Its strength, tenacity and willingness to fight larger animals appealed to 18th-century political cartoonists, who began depicting the female figure of Britannia being accompanied by both a lion and bulldog.

As the phrase 'British bulldog spirit', meaning unrelenting courage, had evolved during the 19th century, plucky bulldogs soon became a regular fixture in World War I propaganda posters. But perhaps the most potent symbolism came when Winston Churchill became prime minister. His jowly face, broad body and steadfast determination to overcome powerful Nazi forces in World War II made him an almost living embodiment of the heroic pooch.

**DID YOU KNOW?**

**MYTH OF MAGIC**
During the English Civil War, Royalists claimed that gullible Roundheads thought Prince Rupert's dog, Boy, was a witch's 'familiar' and could catch bullets in his teeth. The Roundheads didn't – but some history books still think they did!

# Did **Dick Whittington** have a cat?

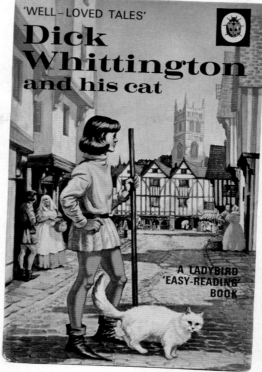

'WELL-LOVED TALES'

**Dick Whittington and his cat**

A LADYBIRD 'EASY-READING' BOOK

**CAPITAL GAINS**
The folk tale of the orphan and his cat are based on a real 14th-century mayor

◎ The tale of Dick Whittington and his cat has passed into folklore and pantomime, but it is based on a real 14th-century merchant and mayor. Ballads and plays – the oldest known examples dating back to the early 17th century – describe an impoverished orphan making his fortune in London after his beloved cat is bought by a foreign king. He promptly marries his master's daughter, Alice, and becomes Lord Mayor of London.

The real Richard Whittington (c1350–1423) was the son of a Gloucestershire landowner. After training as a mercer in London, he made his name by supplying luxury textiles and lending money to the wealthy, including three successive kings: Richard II, Henry IV and Henry V. His wife was indeed called Alice Fitzwarin and he was elected as mayor in 1397, 1406 and 1419 – but there's no mention in the records of a feline companion. This part of the story may derive from other folklore traditions of a man making his fortune with the help of a cat.

Dying a childless widower in 1423, Whittington bequeathed his entire fortune to charity, thus cementing his position as an English folk hero. The somewhat mythical version of his life remained popular all through the Georgian and Victorian eras and is still often seen on stage today.

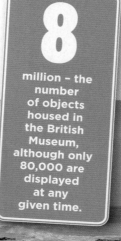

**8** million – the number of objects housed in the British Museum, although only 80,000 are displayed at any given time.

## HOW DID 'LONDON' GET ITS NAME?

◎ During the time of the Romans, the town was known as Londinium and this was passed down to the Saxons as Lundenwic, but the precise origins of the name are unclear. The 12th-century author Geoffrey of Monmouth attributed the founding of London to the mythical King Lud, hence Kaerlud (or 'Lud's City'), while later writers suggested the presence of a Celtic war-leader by the name of Londinos.

It may represent a (Latin) corruption of a named British settlement on the banks of the Thames, or it may have derived from a native term for a geographical feature – for example, the Welsh for a lake or pond (*llyn*).

## When was Britain **last invaded**?

◎ Most people think the answer is 1066, but it's not. The French invaded England in 1216 at the request of the barons fighting King John, though since the barons were themselves French, this invasion wasn't quite as foreign as it looked. During the Irish rebellion against Queen Elizabeth (1594-1603), a small Spanish force landed briefly at Kinsale to help the rebels. Some historians claim that William of Orange's landing in 1688 at the head of a Dutch

**BORDER CONTROL**
Invaders have tried their luck more recently than you might think

army was the last successful foreign invasion of England but, since he'd been invited by Parliament, not everyone agrees. In 1796, a large French invasion force was only beaten back from Bantry Bay in Ireland by bad weather, and two years later the French landed and won the Battle of Castlebar before being forced to surrender to the British. A small French force, led by a not very competent Irish-American, landed near Fishguard in west Wales in 1797, got drunk and were promptly rounded up – 12 of them by a feisty local lady called Jemima Nicholas. In their befuddled state, the French had mistaken the women's traditional red shawls and black hats for advancing British infantry!

**WELSH REBELS**
Angry Chartists battle armed soldiers in Newport

# When was the last armed revolt in Britain?

◎ The famous Newport Rising, which occurred in Monmouthshire in 1839, was an ugly offshoot of the Chartist movement demanding the vote for working-class men. Though action was long planned, the revolt quickly escalated when key Welsh Chartists were detained in a Newport hotel. Hearing this, an armed mob of as many as 5,000 went to liberate them, opening fire on the local yeomanry. The soldiers retaliated, killing around 20, and the mob soon fled in panic. The ringleaders were sentenced to death, but this was later commuted to transportation. Some contemporary conspiracy theorists feared that this uprising was just the beginning of a sinister Russian invasion plot and that the whole nation would soon be under attack.

# WHERE IS OLIVER CROMWELL'S HEAD?

◎ When the Royalists came back to power in 1660 when the monarchy was restored, they dug up Oliver Cromwell's body, hanged it and stuck his head on a spike over Westminster Hall for all to see.

The head eventually fell off the spike and, by the 18th century, it was circulating as a curio: there was a trade at the time in the body parts of (dead) famous people. Cromwell's noggin passed through various hands before ending up with the Wilkinson family in Kent. There it was photographed and examined closely before it was declared genuine. Its authenticity was partly proven by warts. The decaying head still held roots of warts that matched up to those depicted in the Lord Protector's portrait.

In 1960, the head was passed to Cromwell's old college of Sidney Sussex College, Cambridge. To avoid it being targeted by royalists or Irish people, who each have their own reasons to hate Cromwell, the head was buried in the college antechapel but without anything to mark exactly where.

**GETTING A HEAD**
RIGHT: **Oliver Cromwell's eerie death mask**
FAR RIGHT: **Cromwell's head is today buried at a secret spot in Sidney Sussex College, Cambridge**

# WHO WAS THE WEALTHIEST BRITON EVER?

◎ After adjusting for inflation to allow a level playing field, Britain has never known individual wealth like that seized by William the Conqueror after 1066. As king, he nominally owned everything, making him a multi-billionaire, able to dish out staggering rewards to his family and the nobles who supported his claim to the crown. For instance, Alan Rufus, William's nephew, had helped suppress Saxon rebellion in the north, and was presented with 250,000 acres of land for his pains. On his death, Rufus was worth £11,000 – or £81 billion in today's money.

**KING OF BLING**
The wealth of William I is thought to have been in excess of £100 billion

# Who was the first-ever British prime minister?

◎ This is a bit of a trick question. Technically, Britain's first prime minister was Sir Henry Campbell-Bannerman, a Glaswegian Liberal who led from 1905 until ill-health forced him to resign in 1908. This might surprise you, but the truth is that, until 1905, the term 'prime minister' was only a commonly used nickname and the role was officially titled First Lord of the Treasury.

In fact, the term 'prime minister' had originated in the early 18th century as something of an insult. With George I speaking only broken English, and the financial crisis of the South Sea Bubble threatening the economy, British politics was in a perilous state. In 1721, Sir Robert Walpole stepped into the power vacuum and set about cleaning up the mess. His affronted rivals snarkily referred to him as 'prime minister', jealous that he held sway over the king.

**TIME OF THE PM**
The title of 'prime minister' was made official while Sir Henry Campbell-Bannerman was in office

**REMEMBER, DISMEMBER...**
After he was caught, Guy Fawkes was tortured to reveal his co-conspirators

# WHAT IF GUY FAWKES HAD SUCCEEDED?

We still do not know exactly what the Gunpowder plotters hoped to achieve by destroying Parliament. They were Catholics who had recently faced a major clampdown, so they presumably hoped to strike a blow in retaliation. It is possible they wanted a Catholic monarch to replace King James I, though such a violent terrorist plot was unlikely to gain support for a Catholic king. A controlled experiment in 2005, to mark the 400th anniversary of the plot, showed that the amount of gunpowder Fawkes smuggled into Parliament could easily have destroyed the House of Lords and killed everyone in it, including the king, the entire political class and the leadership of the Church. This would have created a huge and dangerous power vacuum and it's not fanciful to believe that this, in turn, could easily have led to a power struggle, almost certainly to civil war and quite possibly foreign invasion. The Spanish, French and Scots could all have seized the opportunity to intervene. With memories of the Spanish Armada only 17 years earlier still fresh, it's no wonder that people celebrated so vociferously when the plot was foiled.

## WHICH CAME FIRST: OXFORD OR CAMBRIDGE?

The older of the two 'great universities' is Oxford. The city can trace the origins of its university institutions to 1167 when King Henry II banned English students from attending the University of Paris. The fact that students set up base in Oxford suggests some organised teaching was already going on there. The young students, however, didn't get on too well with the townspeople. In 1209, two or three were unjustly hanged following the murder of a townswoman, causing many students to flee Oxford and make for Cambridge.

## How old is the national anthem?

Even though Commonwealth countries have their own anthems, *God Save The Queen* is still an official song

Strangely enough, the origins of the British national anthem are shrouded in doubt. Although the phrase 'God save the king, Long live the king' goes back to Saxon times, the song's verses arrived much later. The melody came first, possibly as a Tudor plainsong, or chant. The earliest musical manuscript evidence was written around 1619 by Dr John Bull, who was a famed English organist living in Belgian exile following a sex scandal. Later, the English composer Henry Purcell used bits of the classic refrain in pieces that featured the words "God save the king", while the German George Frideric Handel also borrowed the tune. All have been variously described as the anthem's composer.

We know that the words and music were sung in combination at the Drury Lane Theatre in 1745, having recently been published in *The Gentleman's Magazine*. This performance was a patriotic response to the Scottish Jacobite victory over George II's soldiers at the Battle of Prestopans, with the crowd getting behind the incumbent Hanoverian king against his Catholic Stuart rival for the throne. An extra verse was temporarily added to ram the point home: "May he sedition hush, and like a torrent rush, Rebellious Scots to crush, God save the king!" Bizarrely, however, there is reason to believe that at the same time, *God Save The King* was also a Jacobite drinking anthem, meaning mortal enemies sang the same words to the same tune.

Today, the anthem can still cause confusion as the melody is used in the patriotic songs of other nations, most notably the United States' *My Country, 'Tis of Thee* and Liechtenstein's national anthem. To add further complexity, it's not even the official anthem of Britain; it's merely sung out of customary tradition. As Wales, Northern Ireland and Scotland have their own national anthems, the English sometimes prefer to belt out a chorus of *Jerusalem* or *Land Of Hope And Glory* instead.

## GRAPHIC HISTORY
### London's greatest landmark

# WHAT'S THE STORY OF ST PAUL'S CATHEDRAL?

### "AT ALL COSTS, ST PAUL'S MUST BE SAVED"
WINSTON CHURCHILL, 1940

## TIMELINE

**AD 604**
The site's **first cathedral** is built by Mellitus, an East Saxon.

**AD 675**
A **fire devastates** the first building, but it is quickly rebuilt.

**AD 962**
**Viking invaders** destroy the second cathedral, and a third is constructed out of stone.

**1087**
The Normans aim to make the world's **tallest Christian church** on the site. It is completed in 1240.

**1512**
**St Paul's School** is founded by the cathedral's dean, John Colet.

**1561**
The cathedral's once-record-breaking tall spire collapses after being **hit by lightning**.

**1666**
St Paul's, along with much of the city, is devastated by the **Great Fire of London**.

**1711**
The new St Paul's, designed by Christopher Wren, is officially **declared complete**.

**1882**
Great Paul the bell, which **weighs 17,001kgs**, is hung in the tower.

**1913**
Suffragettes **plant a bomb** under the bishop's throne, but it is not detonated.

**1940**
St Paul's survives **the bombings of World War II** and becomes a symbol of British defiance.

### OPERATION HOPE NOT
Not many funerals have a codename, but Winston Churchill's did. On 30 January 1965, the great wartime leader was laid to rest, after a state service at St Paul's.

## IN THE CRYPT

**CHRISTOPHER WREN**
architect of St Paul's, buried 1723

**LORD NELSON**
naval commander, buried 1805

**JOSEPH TURNER**
painter, buried 1851

**DUKE OF WELLINGTON**
prime minister, buried 1852

**ALEXANDER FLEMING**
biologist, buried 1955

St Paul's has become the eternal resting place for many of Britain's most-respected citizens. As well as war heroes, great politicians, esteemed architects, and artists, including those listed on the left, a walk around the sacred site will also reveal the graves of numerous authors, composers, philosophers and more.

### PEACE OF FRUIT
Gilt pineapples top each of the western towers, as the exotic fruit symbolises peace, prosperity and hospitality.

### OLD BONES
The oldest-known grave at the site belonged to King Æthelred the Unready, who was buried at the third incarnation of the cathedral, in 1016.

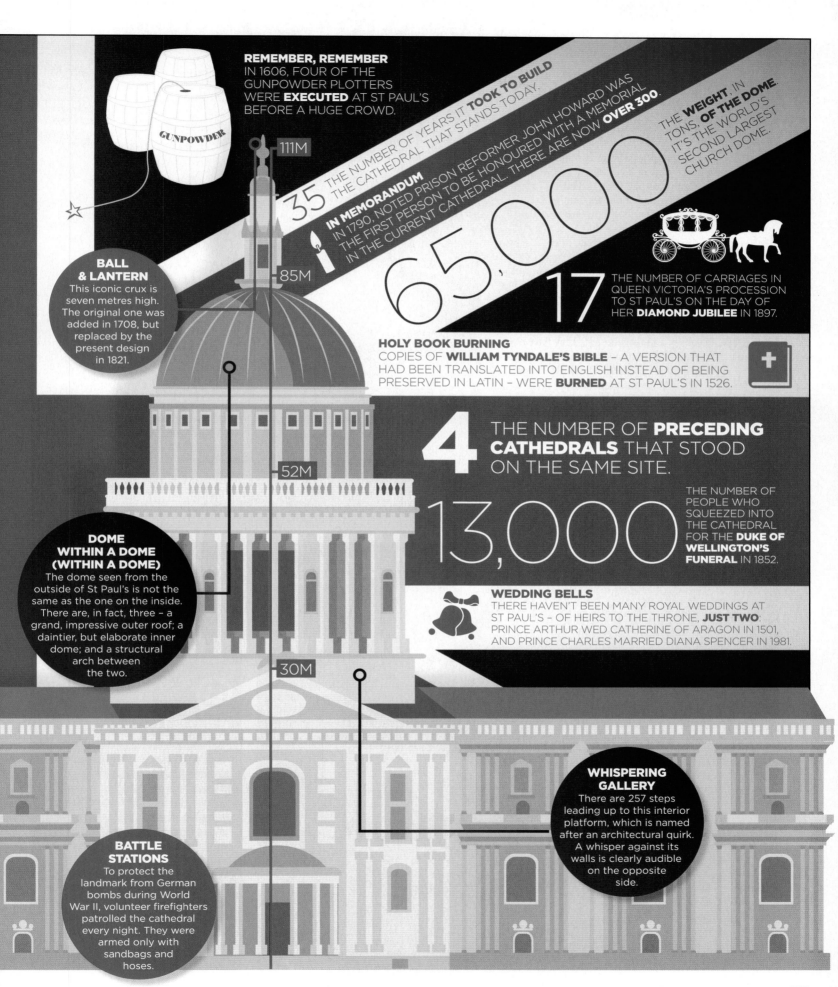

**REMEMBER, REMEMBER**
IN 1606, FOUR OF THE GUNPOWDER PLOTTERS WERE **EXECUTED** AT ST PAUL'S BEFORE A HUGE CROWD.

GUNPOWDER

111M

85M

**35** THE NUMBER OF YEARS IT **TOOK TO BUILD** THE CATHEDRAL THAT STANDS TODAY.

**IN MEMORANDUM** IN 1790, NOTED PRISON REFORMER JOHN HOWARD WAS THE FIRST PERSON TO BE HONOURED WITH A MEMORIAL IN THE CURRENT CATHEDRAL. THERE ARE NOW **OVER 300**.

**65,000** THE **WEIGHT**, IN TONS, **OF THE DOME**. IT'S THE WORLD'S SECOND LARGEST CHURCH DOME.

**BALL & LANTERN**
This iconic crux is seven metres high. The original one was added in 1708, but replaced by the present design in 1821.

**17** THE NUMBER OF CARRIAGES IN QUEEN VICTORIA'S PROCESSION TO ST PAUL'S ON THE DAY OF HER **DIAMOND JUBILEE** IN 1897.

**HOLY BOOK BURNING**
COPIES OF **WILLIAM TYNDALE'S BIBLE** – A VERSION THAT HAD BEEN TRANSLATED INTO ENGLISH INSTEAD OF BEING PRESERVED IN LATIN – WERE **BURNED** AT ST PAUL'S IN 1526.

52M

**4** THE NUMBER OF **PRECEDING CATHEDRALS** THAT STOOD ON THE SAME SITE.

**13,000** THE NUMBER OF PEOPLE WHO SQUEEZED INTO THE CATHEDRAL FOR THE **DUKE OF WELLINGTON'S FUNERAL** IN 1852.

**DOME WITHIN A DOME (WITHIN A DOME)**
The dome seen from the outside of St Paul's is not the same as the one on the inside. There are, in fact, three – a grand, impressive outer roof; a daintier, but elaborate inner dome; and a structural arch between the two.

**WEDDING BELLS**
THERE HAVEN'T BEEN MANY ROYAL WEDDINGS AT ST PAUL'S – OF HEIRS TO THE THRONE, **JUST TWO**: PRINCE ARTHUR WED CATHERINE OF ARAGON IN 1501, AND PRINCE CHARLES MARRIED DIANA SPENCER IN 1981.

30M

**WHISPERING GALLERY**
There are 257 steps leading up to this interior platform, which is named after an architectural quirk. A whisper against its walls is clearly audible on the opposite side.

**BATTLE STATIONS**
To protect the landmark from German bombs during World War II, volunteer firefighters patrolled the cathedral every night. They were armed only with sandbags and hoses.

# Did **Roman Britain** have its own emperor?

◎ Briefly, yes. In AD 286, Rome issued orders for the execution of one of its naval commanders. Carausius had been tasked with clearing the English Channel of pirates, but he was suspected of collaborating with them in order to line his own pockets. When he got wind of his death sentence, Carausius responded by declaring himself Emperor of Britain and northern Gaul (France). To pay his forces and promote his rule, Carausius minted thousands of coins. Many have been uncovered in archaeological excavations and depict a thick-set bruiser of a man with a beard and double chin. Many of what we now call the 'Forts of the Saxon Shore' – Roman forts like Pevensey and Portchester – may have been built, or at least strengthened, by Carausius, not to keep out Saxon raiders, but to defend his empire.

In AD 293, Carausius was assassinated by his finance minister, a man named Allectus who ruled for three years before Rome mounted an invasion, defeated and killed him.

**BIG SPENDER**
**With a double chin, the likeness of Carausius wasn't all that flattering**

# DID THE THAMES REALLY USED TO FREEZE OVER?

**160**

The height in metres of Lincoln Cathedral's medieval spire. Until the spire's 1549 collapse, the cathedral was Europe's tallest building.

The Frost Fair of 1683-4 featured horse racing, bear-baiting and puppet shows on the frozen Thames. It was described as a "carnival on the water"

◎ Yes. In fact, the Thames froze at London at least 23 times between 1408 and 1814. The freezing of the river in the capital, where ice is now rarely seen, was caused by three factors. First, the climate in Britain was on average about 1°C colder between about 1400 and 1800 than before or since. Second, the Thames was then wider and shallower than it is today, as it is now restricted between solid embankments. Finally, the numerous narrow arches of the medieval London Bridge partially blocked the water on the upstream side, reducing the flow. During the big chill of 1683-4, the Thames froze for two months (with ice some 28cm thick), providing a stage for the most famous of the London Frost Fairs.

# Why does the **flag of Wales** feature a red dragon?

◎ The red dragon of Wales dates back to Roman times. Roman cavalry units carried a standard known as the 'draco', or dragon. This took the form of a metal dragon's head with an open mouth, through which the wind would blow. The body of the dragon was made up of a tube of fabric, rather like a modern wind sock. The banners were used both to serve as markers on which the riders formed into different formations and to give orders by means of vigorous waving. The British militias adopted many aspects of Roman military gear and the draco standard was among those taken up with alacrity.

Following the fall of Rome, British princes continued to use Roman-style dracos as battle standards. The last recorded use of the draco by a British army was in about 1250, after which the red dragon of Wales began to be embroidered onto a flag as if it were a heraldic device. The green and white background, incidentally, comes from the family colours of the Tudor dynasty and were added in 1959.

**FIRE BREATHER**
**It might be synonymous with Wales now, but the red dragon has much more distant roots**

# WHY IS BRITAIN CALLED 'GREAT'?

◎ During the fifth and sixth centuries, there was a mass migration of Celts as they fled the political and military turmoil raging in southern Britain – what the Romans called 'Britannia'. They settled in northwestern Gaul (France) in an area soon known as 'Britannia minor', or 'Lesser Britain', after its new inhabitants. It would later become the independent kingdom, and then Duchy, of Brittany. With the union of Scotland and England in 1707, the title 'Kingdom of Great Britain' was officially adopted to describe the new super-state.

## WHY DOES BRITAIN HAVE SO MANY ACCENTS?

◎ As an island, Britain has juggled two conflicting influences on its languages. A constant inflow of global cultures has brought new words and phrases while, until the late 20th century, little mass travel saw individual regions remaining close-knit. So early settlers – Romans, Anglo-Saxons, Norsemen, people from the Germanic countries – brought their languages with them, while the Celtic tongues of Wales, Scotland, Ireland and Cornwall stayed discrete.

Scholars also studied Ancient Greek, the legal system conversed (from 1066) in French, and the language of the church was Latin. The language of ordinary people thus became an ever-evolving dog's dinner of everything, with regions developing their own blends and words. London's dialects pretty much changed with every ship that docked.

Also, before modern transport, people were less mobile. Dialects and accents in each area were steeped in their own rich variations – the same, yet different from the rest of the British Isles.

◎ The British climate may be notoriously awful, but it's not catastrophically so. There have, however, been times of extreme weather. During the third millennium BC, a period of increased warmth and reduced cloud cover seems to have produced bumper harvests; a similar spell in the first century AD attracted the attentions of the Roman Empire.

The worst periods of weather often follow a major volcanic event. In 1816 – the 'year without summer' following Mount Tambora's eruption in Indonesia – volcanic dust blocked the sun, generating near-incessant rainfall that caused harvests to fail and livestock to die. However, the yellow-y tinge to Britain's evening skies may have inspired some of JMW Turner's most-celebrated paintings.

**WEATHER WOES**
What would the British grumble about if not the grey or cloudy weather?

# Has our **weather** always been bad?

**REGAL ROOTS**
The legend of King Arthur lies at the heart of the historic British Empire

### DID YOU KNOW?

**BRITISH BULL**
In 1712, the political caricature 'John Bull' was created. Stocky, plain-spoken and clad in a Union Flag waistcoat, Bull became the archetype of Englishness, but he was actually created by a Scot – mathematician and satirical writer John Arbuthnot.

# HOW OLD IS THE 'BRITISH EMPIRE'?

◎ According to medieval legend, Britain was named after its founding ruler and first king, the Trojan exile Brutus. Following him, others were said to have ruled all of Britain, from Roman Emperor Constantine the Great, to the mythical King Arthur (whose dominions supposedly included England, Wales, Scotland, Ireland, Denmark and France). In the 1500s, when Henry VIII became fascinated by his Arthurian heritage, such ancient ideas began to spring up again. As Wales and Ireland were under English rule, only Scotland stood in the way of a new Britannia. In the 1540s, the pro-alliance James Henrisoun called on fellow Scots to "laie doune their weapons" as "Englande was the onely supreme seat of the empire of greate Briteigne".

It was 50 years later that John Dee – chief astrologer and cartographer to Elizabeth I – also spoke of the "Brytish Empire", but his definition included the newly acquired colonies in North America. As a Welshman aiding a Tudor queen of Welsh ancestry, Dee appealed to the Arthurian notion of an overseas empire. This expansionist understanding of the phrase remained in use throughout the 1600s (though often specified as the 'English Empire') but, in 1707, the Act of Union between England and Scotland officially created the sovereign power of Great Britain. By the mid-1700s, use of 'British Empire' was widespread.

## HOW DID THEY DO THAT?
# THE TAJ MAHAL

### The marble marvel is the world's most famous monument to love

The Taj Mahal is famous for being the mausoleum of Arjumand Banu Begum – best known as Mumtaz Mahal, favourite wife of Mughal Emperor Shah Jahan – who died giving birth to her 14th child. But though her domed white marble tomb is the centrepiece, the Taj is actually a complex of buildings and grounds, artfully blending Islamic, Persian, Hindu and Ottoman styles. Built between 1631 and 1653 by the banks of the Yamuna River in the city of Agra, the construction of the Taj Mahal involved some 20,000 workers and incorporated materials from China, Tibet, Sri Lanka and Arabia.

### DOME AND FINIAL
The white marble dome is 35m high, but seems taller, sitting on a 7m-high drum. Like the *chhattris*, *minarets* and *guldastas*, it's topped with a lotus design and bronze finial (replacing the original gold finial).

### GULDASTA
Tall, slender *guldastas* – decorative spires – rise from the edges of the mausoleum's walls.

### SITE MAP
1 Mausoleum
2 Mosque
3 Mihmankhana (guesthouse)
4 Charbagh (formal garden)
5 Darwaza-i-Rauza (Great Gate)
6 Jilaukhana (forecourt)
7 Khawasspuras (tomb attendants' quarters)
8 Saheli Burj (subsidiary tombs)
9 Outer gate to Taj Ganj

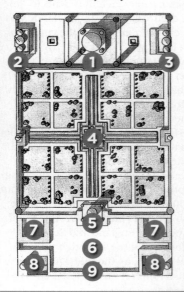

### DECORATION
Islam prohibits images of living creatures, so the decorations – created with paint, stucco, inlays or carving – comprise calligraphy, plant forms or abstract patterns.

### CHHATTRI
Four open-sided *chattris* (kiosks) surround the central dome. Their open bases allow light into the interior of the mausoleum.

### THE PLINTH
The base of the mausoleum is unusually high, ensuring that it stands taller than surrounding structures.

ILLUSTRATION: SOL 90, GETTY X1, ISTOCK X1

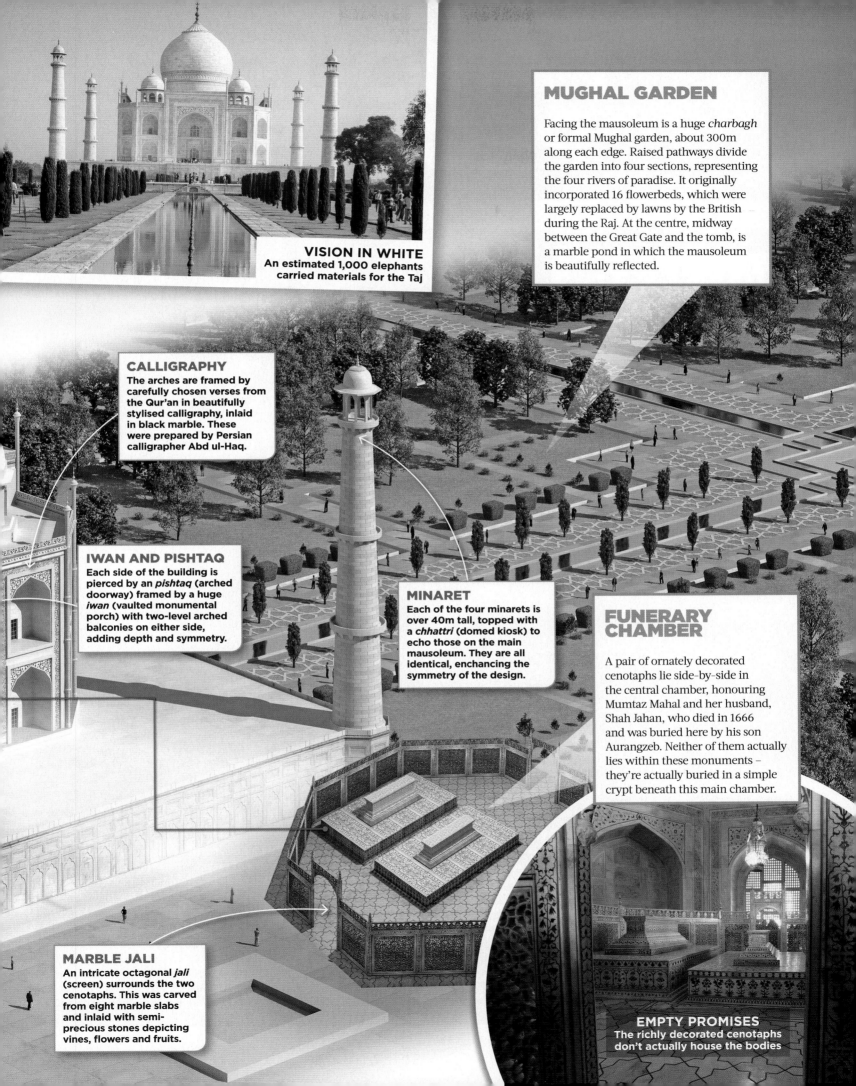

## MUGHAL GARDEN

Facing the mausoleum is a huge *charbagh* or formal Mughal garden, about 300m along each edge. Raised pathways divide the garden into four sections, representing the four rivers of paradise. It originally incorporated 16 flowerbeds, which were largely replaced by lawns by the British during the Raj. At the centre, midway between the Great Gate and the tomb, is a marble pond in which the mausoleum is beautifully reflected.

### VISION IN WHITE
An estimated 1,000 elephants carried materials for the Taj

## CALLIGRAPHY

The arches are framed by carefully chosen verses from the Qur'an in beautifully stylised calligraphy, inlaid in black marble. These were prepared by Persian calligrapher Abd ul-Haq.

## IWAN AND PISHTAQ

Each side of the building is pierced by an *pishtaq* (arched doorway) framed by a huge *iwan* (vaulted monumental porch) with two-level arched balconies on either side, adding depth and symmetry.

## MINARET

Each of the four minarets is over 40m tall, topped with a *chhattri* (domed kiosk) to echo those on the main mausoleum. They are all identical, enchancing the symmetry of the design.

## FUNERARY CHAMBER

A pair of ornately decorated cenotaphs lie side-by-side in the central chamber, honouring Mumtaz Mahal and her husband, Shah Jahan, who died in 1666 and was buried here by his son Aurangzeb. Neither of them actually lies within these monuments – they're actually buried in a simple crypt beneath this main chamber.

## MARBLE JALI

An intricate octagonal *jali* (screen) surrounds the two cenotaphs. This was carved from eight marble slabs and inlaid with semi-precious stones depicting vines, flowers and fruits.

### EMPTY PROMISES
The richly decorated cenotaphs don't actually house the bodies

## WAS **MAID MARIAN** REAL?

**UNLIKELY PAIR**
Marian and Robin's romance is about as plausible as Kevin Costner's accent in *Robin Hood: Prince of Thieves*

◎ Maid Marian is best known today as the legendary love of the equally legendary outlaw Robin Hood. However, the two did not come together until some generations after they both died. While Robin Hood is thought by some to have been an outlaw in the later 13th century, Marian (or Matilda as she may have been named) was daughter to Earl Robert Fitzwalter some 50 years earlier. In 1211, she was living at court in order to learn courtly manners, meet eligible suitors and otherwise finish her education.

While there, she attracted the unwelcome attentions of King John who made a clumsy effort to seduce her. Marian fled to her father, who promptly joined the barons opposed to King John's arbitrary rule. Fitzwalter was not only a powerful baron in his own right, but his influence brought the wealthy merchants of London and other cities onto the rebel side. Their money allowed the rebels to stay in the field while King John's army could not and so secured the agreement known as Magna Carta. Marian's role in forcing Magna Carta on

King John ensured her fame. She became the heroine of various songs and stories.

At some point, Lady Marian got conflated with the rather less virginal, less noble figure of Marian of May. This shepherdess was a stock figure in the rustic revels and plays that took place on May Day. She was romantically linked to the outlaw Robin Hood by about 1500. By 1600, the two Marians had become one, with the shepherdess Marian incorrectly identified as Lady Marian Fitzwalter in hiding from the lecherous King John.

# Did Abraham Lincoln's beard
## win him the election?

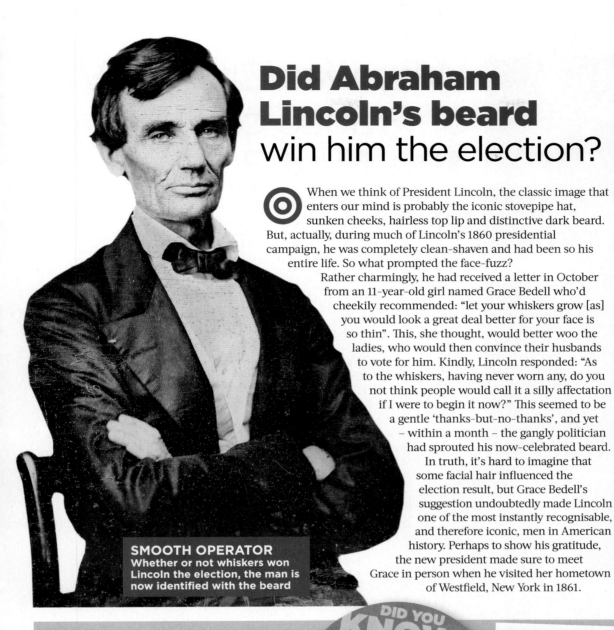

**SMOOTH OPERATOR**
Whether or not whiskers won Lincoln the election, the man is now identified with the beard

◎ When we think of President Lincoln, the classic image that enters our mind is probably the iconic stovepipe hat, sunken cheeks, hairless top lip and distinctive dark beard. But, actually, during much of Lincoln's 1860 presidential campaign, he was completely clean-shaven and had been so his entire life. So what prompted the face-fuzz?

Rather charmingly, he had received a letter in October from an 11-year-old girl named Grace Bedell who'd cheekily recommended: "let your whiskers grow [as] you would look a great deal better for your face is so thin". This, she thought, would better woo the ladies, who would then convince their husbands to vote for him. Kindly, Lincoln responded: "As to the whiskers, having never worn any, do you not think people would call it a silly affectation if I were to begin it now?" This seemed to be a gentle 'thanks-but-no-thanks', and yet – within a month – the gangly politician had sprouted his now-celebrated beard.

In truth, it's hard to imagine that some facial hair influenced the election result, but Grace Bedell's suggestion undoubtedly made Lincoln one of the most instantly recognisable, and therefore iconic, men in American history. Perhaps to show his gratitude, the new president made sure to meet Grace in person when he visited her hometown of Westfield, New York in 1861.

## DID LORD BYRON REALLY HAVE A PET BEAR?

◎ Among the many other eccentricities of the Romantic poet, Lord Byron did indeed keep a bear as a pet. He was a noted animal lover and so was annoyed when he became a student at Trinity College, Cambridge, in 1805, only to be told that the college banned the keeping of pet dogs. Byron brought along a tame bear instead, arguing that bears weren't specifically mentioned in the college statutes so there were no legal grounds for complaint. Byron won the argument and the bear was allowed to stay in his room.

## DID MARIE ANTOINETTE REALLY SAY "LET THEM EAT CAKE"?

**DID YOU KNOW?**

**IN HOT WATER**
Winston Churchill planned strategies – and conducted meetings – in the bath. He once emerged before a startled President Roosevelt saying: "The Prime Minister has nothing to hide from the President of the United States."

◎ If she did utter these words, she was being terribly unoriginal. Although its true provenance is uncertain, this attack on privilege existed long before the revolution and was only attributed to the French queen 50 years after her execution.

According to historian Nancy Barker, it was "an old chestnut" in criticism of women from the House of Bourbon, including Louis XV's daughters.

Philosopher Jean-Jacques Rousseau wrote a very similar anecdote about a "great princess" five years before Marie Antoinette arrived in France.

While it was reported that a cruel politician snarled "let them eat hay", there is no evidence that revolutionaries levelled this familiar accusation against Marie Antoinette. The earliest known source for this enduring myth is a French journal of 1843.

**CRUMBS! IT'S THE QUEEN**
Marie Antoinette never actually condemned her people to a life of over-indulgence at the bakery

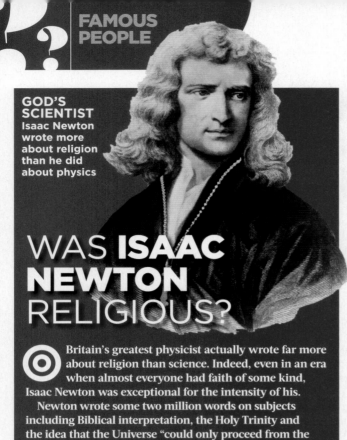

**GOD'S SCIENTIST**
Isaac Newton wrote more about religion than he did about physics

# WAS ISAAC NEWTON RELIGIOUS?

◎ Britain's greatest physicist actually wrote far more about religion than science. Indeed, even in an era when almost everyone had faith of some kind, Isaac Newton was exceptional for the intensity of his.

Newton wrote some two million words on subjects including Biblical interpretation, the Holy Trinity and the idea that the Universe "could only proceed from the counsel and dominion of an intelligent and powerful being". Though he possessed some radical, almost heretical views, he also wrote strongly to condemn atheism, and argued that ancient temples – such as Stonehenge – had been built along heavenly patterns in the worship of the creator God. Most surprising of all, Newton pored over Biblical texts looking for clues prophesying future events and predicted that the Apocalypse would come in the year 2060.

# Why was Charles VI of France called 'the Mad'?

◎ Crowned at the age of 11 in 1380, Charles VI of France was much loved as a benevolent king in his early reign. But while travelling with a retinue of knights in 1392, he suffered the first of many psychological breakdowns. A leper stopped him on the road and warned him that he was about to be betrayed, and then a subsequent loud noise triggered a violent fit of madness. The King lashed out with his sword, killing at least one knight before being restrained.

Sadly, this was the first of 44 bouts of insanity, each lasting between three and nine months, until his death in 1422.

Famously, his symptoms included the Glass Delusion – a belief that he was made of glass and would shatter if touched. His behaviour earned the moniker, 'the Mad'.

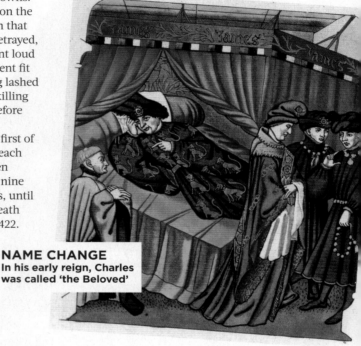

**NAME CHANGE**
In his early reign, Charles was called 'the Beloved'

**DID YOU KNOW?**
**OUT FOR THE COUNT**
Inspired by the campaign for the vote, in 1911 hundreds of women defaced their census forms or hid from the enumerator. Suffragette Emily Wilding Davison was only counted after being found hiding in a House of Commons cupboard.

# DID CHURCHILL HAVE ANY HOBBIES?

◎ The workaholic Sir Winston Churchill famously relaxed by painting – a hobby he'd started in 1915 after the disastrous Gallipoli campaign – and visitors to his Kent home, Chartwell, can view many of his canvases. But also visible is a red brick wall in his garden, which Winston proudly laid "with his own hands" between 1925-32. The future war leader was a dedicated member of the Amalgamated Union of Bricklayers and could lay 200 bricks a day.

**VAN BUREN**
Over 60 years after the US was formed, the first 'American' President was sworn in

# Who was the first US-born president?

◎ On 4 July 1776, the 13 American colonies declared independence from Britain and bound themselves together as the United States. In 1789, this new nation elected its first president, George Washington, but the next six leaders would not be American-born citizens, because they had entered the world as subjects to the British Crown.

It was in 1837, the year of Queen Victoria's enthronement, that Martin Van Buren (born in 1782) became president number eight and broke the link to the royalist past. Yet, while he may have been the first American-born, he actually grew up speaking Dutch.

**GREAT SCOT**
The fictional English sleuth Sherlock Holmes was based on a Scottish professor

## WAS SHERLOCK HOLMES BASED ON A REAL PERSON?

◎ Despite appearing quintessentially English, the super-sleuthing Sherlock was created by a Scottish doctor with Irish parents, and was inspired by another famous Scot. As a 17-year-old medical student in Edinburgh, Arthur Conan Doyle first met Dr Joseph Bell, a man he later described as being able to "diagnose the people as they came in, before they even opened their mouths. He would tell them details of their past life; and hardly would he ever make a mistake". Bell's extraordinary powers of observation made him a leading pioneer in forensic medicine, but also gave author Conan Doyle the foundation for a brilliant character, as he later admitted to his old professor: "You are yourself Sherlock Holmes and well you know it."

**DID YOU KNOW?**
**GOOSE STEP**
In the 1840s, a goose called Jacob was made 'superintendent to the sentinels' of the Coldstream Guards. He'd been enlisted in Quebec after reportedly alerting the regiment to an attack, and brought to the UK as a mascot.

## JUST HOW TALL WAS NAPOLEON?

◎ If there's one thing Napoleon is known for, it's that he was short – and very unhappy about it. There is even a psychological complex named after him. The French leader's diminutive height was mocked relentlessly by English propagandists at the time, but why? He was once described as "a remarkably strong, well-built man, about five feet seven inches high", which was above average height. His image as the 'Little Corporal' was a term of affection from his troops and came from his tendency as a junior officer to micro-manage the battlefield. Yet, his reputation was sealed when he died in 1821. The physician's report gave his height as 5'2" – the note stating this was 'equal to five feet six' by English measurements was conveniently forgotten.

## What happened to Einstein's brain?

◎ Before his death in 1955, Albert Einstein had requested that he be cremated, so his corpse didn't become the plaything of superfans and scientists. Yet the on-duty pathologist, Thomas Harvey, removed Einstein's brain during the eminent physicist's autopsy. Many were outraged, but Harvey convinced Einstein's son to let him keep the brain, promising that it would further the cause of neuroscience. Indeed, he sliced the brain into over 200 pieces, some of which he sent to medical experts in the hope they could find clues to Einstein's brilliance.

However, few were interested in this madcap scheme, so Harvey kept most of the brain, in two jars, inside a beer cooler. Eventually, he tried to pass the bits of brain on to Einstein's granddaughter, but she didn't want them either.

It wasn't until 1978, when a journalist reported Harvey's bizarre quest, that scientists took an interest. But Harvey's DIY approach to preservation likely means any experimental results are flawed. The brain slices are now kept in two American medical museums.

**BONEY MINI**
During the Napoleonic Wars, cartoons relentlessly showed 'Boney' as being very petit

# GRAPHIC HISTORY
Britain's PMs in facts and figures

## WHAT'S THE TYPICAL LIFE OF A BRITISH PRIME MINISTER?

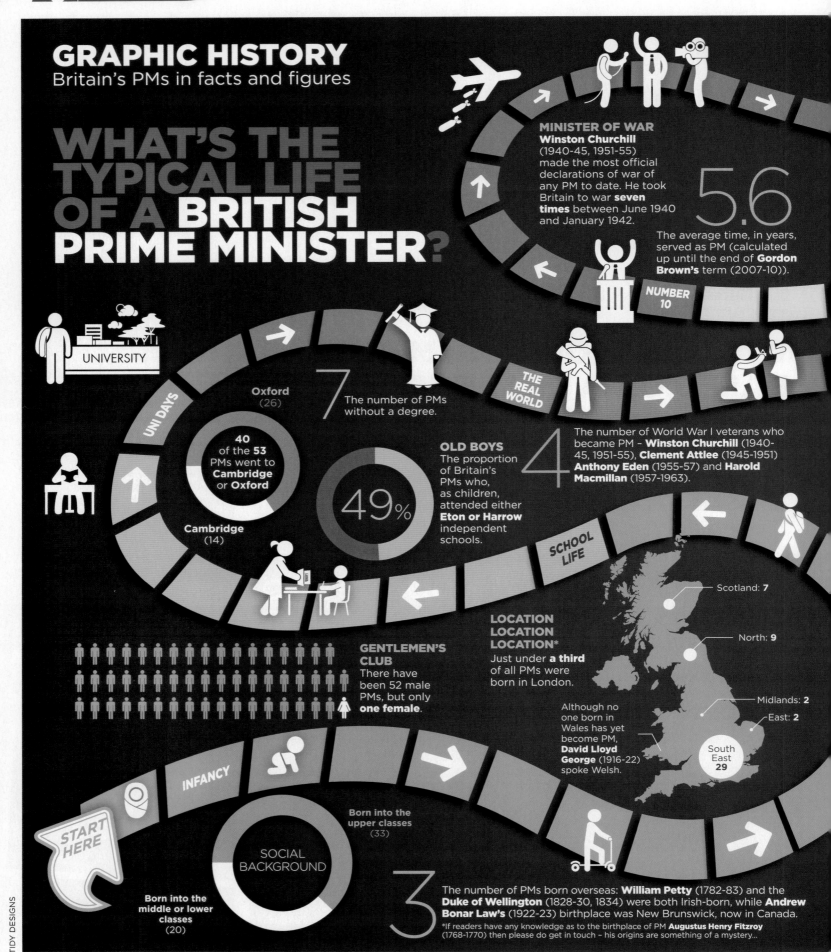

**MINISTER OF WAR**
**Winston Churchill** (1940-45, 1951-55) made the most official declarations of war of any PM to date. He took Britain to war **seven times** between June 1940 and January 1942.

**5.6**
The average time, in years, served as PM (calculated up until the end of **Gordon Brown's** term (2007-10)).

**NUMBER 10**

**UNIVERSITY**

**UNI DAYS**

Oxford (26)

**7** The number of PMs without a degree.

**40** of the **53** PMs went to **Cambridge** or **Oxford**

Cambridge (14)

**THE REAL WORLD**

**4** The number of World War I veterans who became PM – **Winston Churchill** (1940-45, 1951-55), **Clement Attlee** (1945-1951) **Anthony Eden** (1955-57) and **Harold Macmillan** (1957-1963).

**OLD BOYS**
The proportion of Britain's PMs who, as children, attended either **Eton or Harrow** independent schools.

**49%**

**SCHOOL LIFE**

**GENTLEMEN'S CLUB**
There have been 52 male PMs, but only **one female**.

**LOCATION LOCATION LOCATION***
Just under **a third** of all PMs were born in London.

Although no one born in Wales has yet become PM, **David Lloyd George** (1916-22) spoke Welsh.

Scotland: **7**

North: **9**

Midlands: **2**

East: **2**

South East **29**

**INFANCY**

**START HERE**

Born into the upper classes (33)

**SOCIAL BACKGROUND**

Born into the middle or lower classes (20)

**3** The number of PMs born overseas: **William Petty** (1782-83) and the **Duke of Wellington** (1828-30, 1834) were both Irish-born, while **Andrew Bonar Law's** (1922-23) birthplace was New Brunswick, now in Canada.

*If readers have any knowledge as to the birthplace of PM **Augustus Henry Fitzroy** (1768-1770) then please do get in touch – his origins are something of a mystery...

TIDY DESIGNS

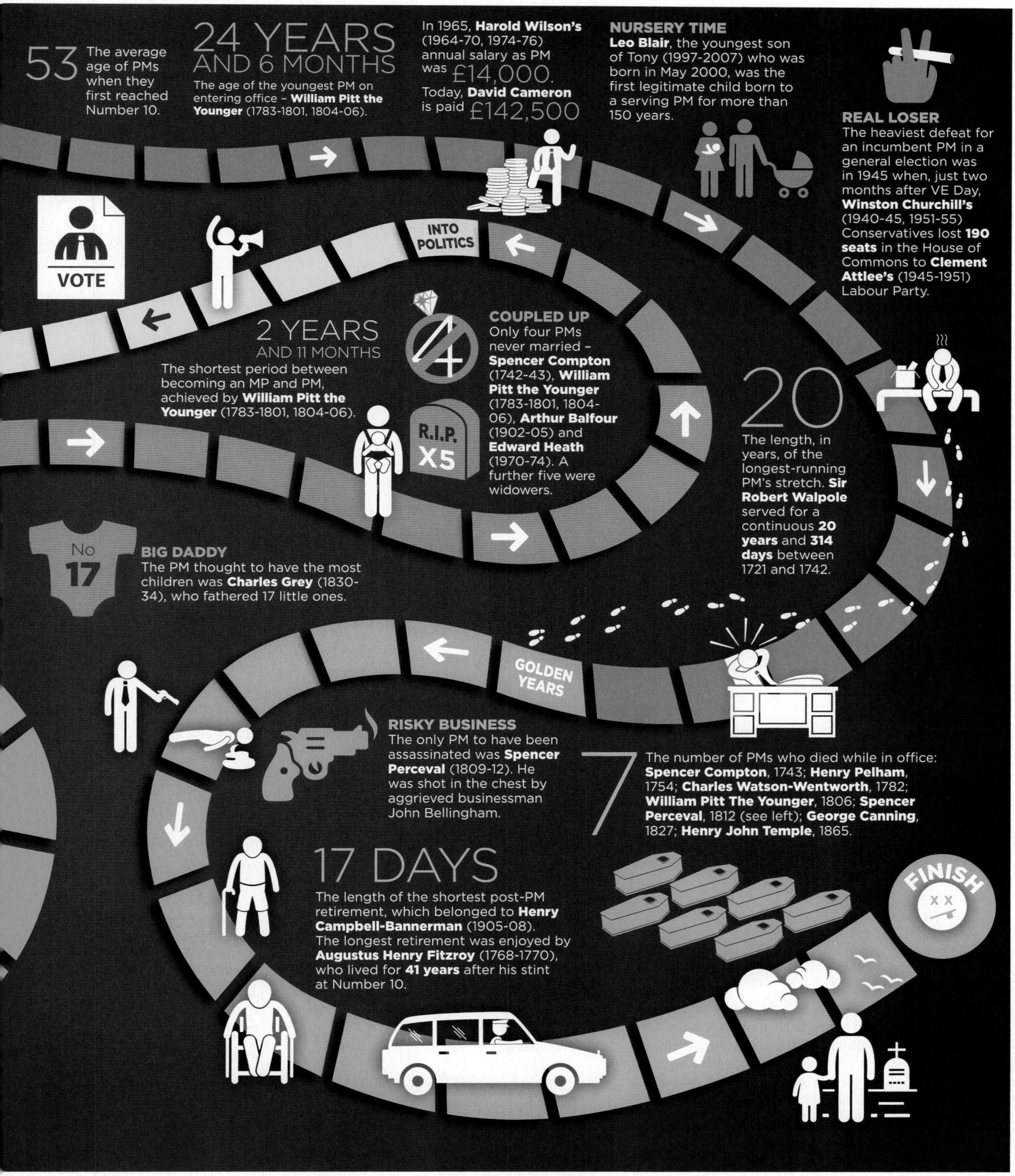

**53** The average age of PMs when they first reached Number 10.

# 24 YEARS
## AND 6 MONTHS
The age of the youngest PM on entering office – **William Pitt the Younger** (1783-1801, 1804-06).

In 1965, **Harold Wilson's** (1964-70, 1974-76) annual salary as PM was **£14,000.** Today, **David Cameron** is paid **£142,500**

**NURSERY TIME**
**Leo Blair**, the youngest son of Tony (1997-2007) who was born in May 2000, was the first legitimate child born to a serving PM for more than 150 years.

**REAL LOSER**
The heaviest defeat for an incumbent PM in a general election was in 1945 when, just two months after VE Day, **Winston Churchill's** (1940-45, 1951-55) Conservatives lost **190 seats** in the House of Commons to **Clement Attlee's** (1945-1951) Labour Party.

**VOTE**

**INTO POLITICS**

# 2 YEARS
## AND 11 MONTHS
The shortest period between becoming an MP and PM, achieved by **William Pitt the Younger** (1783-1801, 1804-06).

**COUPLED UP**
Only four PMs never married – **Spencer Compton** (1742-43), **William Pitt the Younger** (1783-1801, 1804-06), **Arthur Balfour** (1902-05) and **Edward Heath** (1970-74). A further five were widowers.

**R.I.P. X5**

# 20
The length, in years, of the longest-running PM's stretch. **Sir Robert Walpole** served for a continuous **20 years** and **314 days** between 1721 and 1742.

**No 17**
**BIG DADDY**
The PM thought to have the most children was **Charles Grey** (1830-34), who fathered 17 little ones.

**GOLDEN YEARS**

**RISKY BUSINESS**
The only PM to have been assassinated was **Spencer Perceval** (1809-12). He was shot in the chest by aggrieved businessman John Bellingham.

**7** The number of PMs who died while in office: **Spencer Compton**, 1743; **Henry Pelham**, 1754; **Charles Watson-Wentworth**, 1782; **William Pitt The Younger**, 1806; **Spencer Perceval**, 1812 (see left); **George Canning**, 1827; **Henry John Temple**, 1865.

# 17 DAYS
The length of the shortest post-PM retirement, which belonged to **Henry Campbell-Bannerman** (1905-08). The longest retirement was enjoyed by **Augustus Henry Fitzroy** (1768-1770), who lived for **41 years** after his stint at Number 10.

**FINISH**

# WONDERS OF THE WORLD

## HOW DID THEY DO THAT?
# MACHU PICCHU

### The lost city of the Inca, hidden between two Peruvian peaks

◎ Concealed from the Spaniards for centuries, this site was largely unknown to Westerners until 1911, when American professor Hiram Bingham was shown the way by a local. These mysterious pre-Colombian ruins are still little understood. They could be a city – either abandoned when the Spaniards invaded, or merely hidden at that time – a royal retreat, or a sacred site of pilgrimage. Whichever it was, Machu Picchu was definitely a site of great ceremonial significance. The area is divided into two main sectors; the agricultural and the urban section. Near the top is the sacred zone, *Hanan*, while the living accommodation – *Urin* – is mostly found in the lower levels.

**SUN TEMPLE**
A semi-circular tower, used for ceremonies and rituals. One of its windows is designed to frame the sunrise on the longest day of the year, another, the shortest.

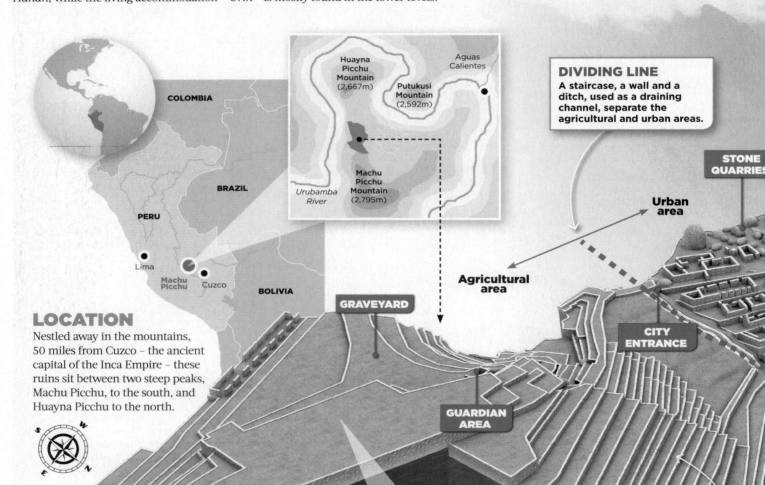

**DIVIDING LINE**
A staircase, a wall and a ditch, used as a draining channel, separate the agricultural and urban areas.

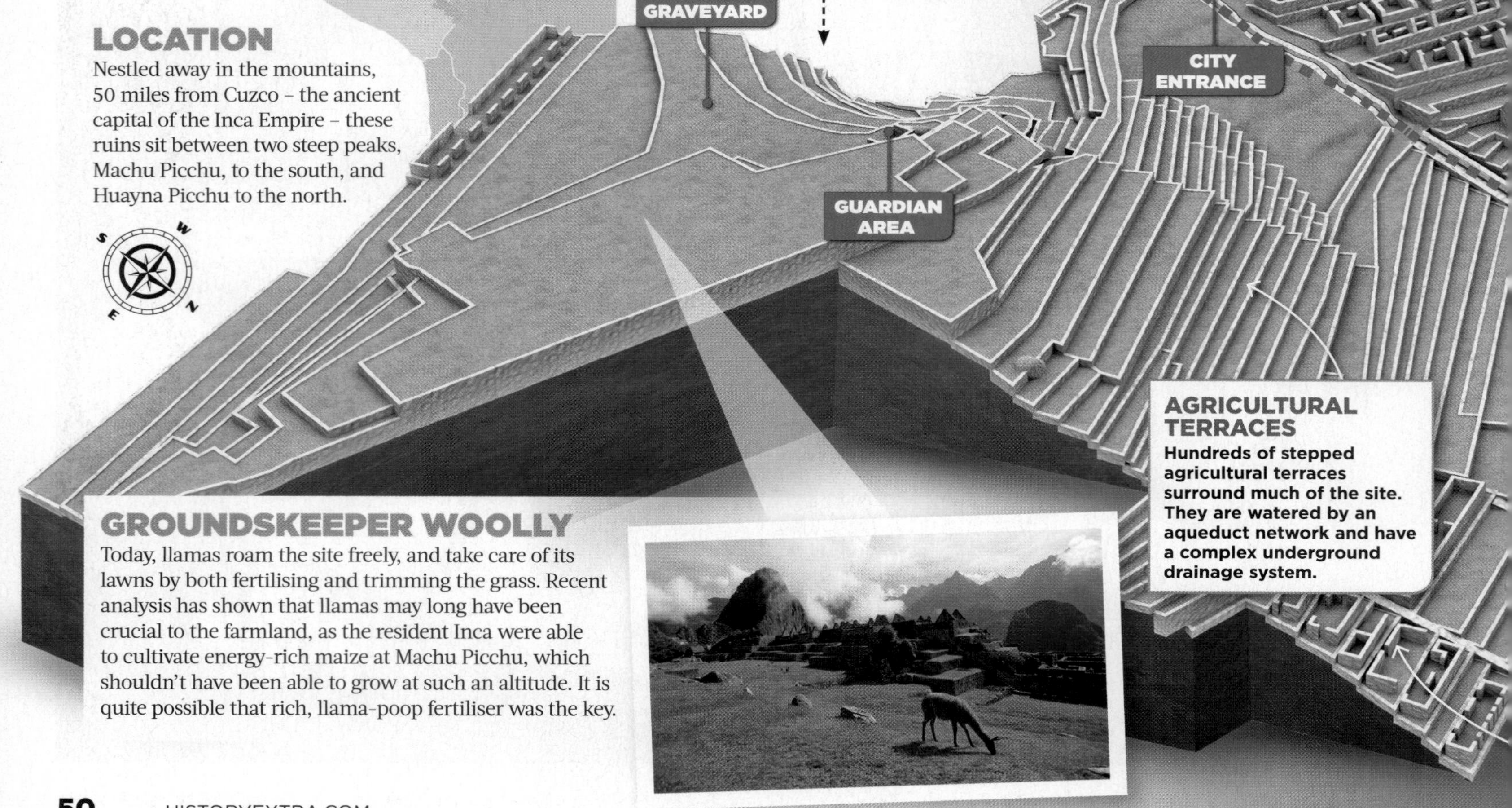

**STONE QUARRIES**

**Urban area**

**Agricultural area**

**GRAVEYARD**

**CITY ENTRANCE**

**GUARDIAN AREA**

### LOCATION
Nestled away in the mountains, 50 miles from Cuzco – the ancient capital of the Inca Empire – these ruins sit between two steep peaks, Machu Picchu, to the south, and Huayna Picchu to the north.

*Map labels:* COLOMBIA, BRAZIL, PERU, BOLIVIA, Lima, Machu Picchu, Cuzco

*Inset map labels:* Huayna Picchu Mountain (2,667m), Putukusi Mountain (2,592m), Aguas Calientes, Urubamba River, Machu Picchu Mountain (2,795m)

### AGRICULTURAL TERRACES
Hundreds of stepped agricultural terraces surround much of the site. They are watered by an aqueduct network and have a complex underground drainage system.

### GROUNDSKEEPER WOOLLY
Today, llamas roam the site freely, and take care of its lawns by both fertilising and trimming the grass. Recent analysis has shown that llamas may long have been crucial to the farmland, as the resident Inca were able to cultivate energy-rich maize at Machu Picchu, which shouldn't have been able to grow at such an altitude. It is quite possible that rich, llama-poop fertiliser was the key.

## SECRET LOCATION
This famous view of the site doesn't actually show the peak of Machu Picchu – it shows Huayna Picchu

## HOME OF KINGS?
Most investigators think it was Pachacuti, Inca empire builder of the 15th century, who ordered the construction of this estate at Machu Picchu. As well as this high-altitude development, it is also thought that Pachacuti devised the city plan for Cuzco, which grew from the size of a hamlet to the capital city of his vast new empire during his lifetime.

## INTIWATANA
The 'hitching post of the Sun', this carved rock pillar was used during solstice ceremonies. It may also have been a solar clock, used to indicate the position of the Sun in solstices, or a sacrificial altar.

**MAIN SQUARE**

**Hanan (sacred area)**

**Urin (residential area)**

**PRIESTS' HOUSE**

**THREE WINDOW TEMPLE**

**MAIN TEMPLE**

**SACRED STONE**

## ROYAL PALACE
Spread over two floors, and with fine masonry, this stately building had multiple rooms.

## FACE OFF
For the Inca, part of Huayna Picchu's appeal was that it was thought to resemble a face in profile, looking up to the sky. The peak is its nose, and the valley to the left, its lips.

**INDUSTRIAL CENTRE**

## ROYAL TOMB
Beneath the Sun Temple lies a rock cave. Symbolic icons including the snake and condor embellish its walls. Although it is commonly referred to as the Royal Tomb, no mummies have ever been uncovered there.

## CONDOR TEMPLE
At this ceremonial centre, a natural rock formation has been carved and shaped to look like a condor in flight. The condor, the largest bird in the world, had great significance for the Inca. It represented the 'upper world', connecting people to their spirit selves. Some historians believe this temple had a sacrificial purpose.

## OUTER TURRETS
On the lower part of the mountain there are five buildings – one on each level. It is thought they served to control one of the city's key access points.

ILLUSTRATION: SOL 90, ALAMY X1, ISTOCK X3

# WHEN DID PEOPLE START WEARING SUNGLASSES?

Experiments with tinted eyewear stretch back for centuries, including lenses made of smoky quartz in 12th-century China and Georgian spectacles designed to correct vision impairment. Silent film stars are also said to have used them to shield their eyes from studio lighting. But the man credited with taking sunglasses from specialist equipment to affordable fashion accessory is founder of the Foster Grant eyewear company, Sam Foster. He began selling his mass-produced shades by the beaches of Atlantic City, New Jersey, in 1929, where they caught on thanks to both the practical benefits and the allure of 'Hollywood glamour'. Drawing on new technologies pioneered for US pilots, Ray-Ban made their distinctive 'aviator' glasses eight years later. By 1938, sunglasses were fashionable enough to be described as a "new fad for wear on city streets" by *Life* magazine.

**SUNNY STYLE**
By the time Doris Riter became an actress in the 1950s, sunnies were a style staple

# Why did Scots start wearing **kilts**?

Kilts are not unique to Scotland. Simple tunics were common in ancient times but, by the medieval period, were associated with backward, more primitive cultures.

In Scotland, clansmen of the Highlands wore a large sort of blanket known as a belted plaid. This was fixed by a belt around the waist as a skirt, and also went over the upper body. Lowlanders, however, thought the belted plaid demonstrated the primitiveness of the Highlanders.

The Highland clans who fought for Bonnie Prince Charlie in 1745 wore the belted plaid, but after his defeat at the Battle of Culloden, the plaid was banned by order of the London government. Meanwhile, a simpler kilt, consisting of a basic pleated skirt attached with a belt, had been developed by an Englishman named Rawlinson

for the workers at his iron foundry at Glengarry. It was adopted for Scottish regiments by the British as an acceptable way of integrating Scottish culture into the British army.

Official approval for the kilt came in 1822, when George IV wore one in Edinburgh. Tartan was a popular pattern for both belted plaid and kilts, but the idea of specific tartans being associated with particular clans is largely a Victorian invention.

**CLAN STYLE**
Kilts aren't as traditional as you might think – and nor is what you choose to wear beneath them

## WHO INVENTED WELLIES?

The Duke of Wellington wore the Hessian boot – a tight-fitting waterproof riding boot that reached to the knee, with a raised peak to protect the front of the knee in battle. Making leather boots waterproof was expensive, but in 1852 industrialist Hiram Hutchinson realised that vulcanised rubber, invented by Charles Goodyear, was the ideal material. He made some in the shape of a short Hessian and called them Wellingtons – and the welly was born.

### DID YOU KNOW?

**WRONG TROUSERS**
To Romans, trousers were the ultimate symbol of the horse-riding barbarian. This suspicion towards such a benign item of clothing lasted until Roman soldiers marched into cold northern Europe and realised the practicality of warm breeches.

**THE SCIENCE BIT**
The Harness Electric Corset contained zinc and copper plates that were said to generate a health-giving current

## What was the **'self-adjusting symmetrico-restorator corporiform'**?

Fashion in the 19th century demanded that women sport tight-fitting corsets that unnaturally squeezed their waists, in extreme instances, to a mere 17 inches. Understandably, this could cause severe medical conditions, including damage to the internal organs, fractured ribs, weakened muscles, reduced fertility and a constant breathlessness that made walking upstairs feel as tough as a mountain trek. Tragically, a few cases were fatal, including those involving young children.

Some Victorian doctors recognised the danger but, in a cruel irony, could do nothing to stop manufacturers touting the dubious medical benefits of specialist models.

The 'self-adjusting symmetrico restorator corporiform' was designed to correct the curved spines of overweight ladies by sucking in the fat and straightening their posture. Meanwhile, skinnier ladies in search of more cleavage could wear the 'Invisible Scapula Contractor', a corset that squeezed inwards from the sides.

Indeed, all manner of body shapes were catered for, but very few corsets would have met modern health and safety standards.

## HOW DID REGENCY LADIES WASH THEIR HAIR?

**In the time of Jane Austen, hair care relied on homemade concoctions. One 'cleanser of the head' from 1811 involved frothing the whites of six eggs into the hair and rinsing with rum and rose water. But having clean hair was perhaps less important than its lustre, which was easily achieved through the application of beef marrow, brandy and unsalted lard. The inevitably less-than-lovely fragrance could be disguised with the use of cinnamon and aniseed perfume.**

**BRIEFER BRIEFS**
Knickers have reduced in size since the days of knickerbockers

# When did knickers start to be worn?

Knickers are relatively new. For centuries, it was practical for ladies to wear only a long shift beneath their skirts – anything akin to gentlemen's pantaloons were considered lewd and uncouth. But the fashions of the 1790s necessitated something more protective of both the woman's body and her modesty, so 19th-century garments fell right to the ankles. As new fabrics, and increased concerns over mobility and hygiene, transformed women's clothing, dresses got smaller – as did the underclothing. Knee-length 'knickerbockers' were common by the 1870s.

**DID YOU KNOW?**
**ROUND THE CLOCK**
Until 1869, all officers of the Metropolitan Police were required to wear their uniforms both on and off duty, including carrying wooden truncheons in the long pockets of their coats.

# Who were the Ton-Up Boys?

With post-war teenagers aching for excitement and post-war A roads comparatively quiet, it was only a matter of time before the two collided. Cars were too expensive for even the newly wealthy young people of the 1950s, so they souped up their motorcycles – and a subculture was born.

Ton-Up Boys, those who could speed their bikes over a 'ton' (100mph), also became known as 'rockers' or 'greasers'. Styling themselves on Marlon Brando in *The Wild One*, they rebelled against authority – and society was outraged. Between death-defying races, 'café racers' hung around transport 'caffs' listening to rock'n'roll music. Most famous of all was the Ace Café in north London, which served coffee, music and greasy-spoon specials until it closed in 1969. After a grass-roots campaign, it re-opened in 1997 and now attracts thousands of bikers from around the world each year.

**ROAR POWER**
Leather-clad 'Ton-Up Boys' were the forerunners of greasers, or rockers

# HOW DID ELIZABETH I USE FASHION TO CREATE HER PUBLIC IMAGE?

## TIMELESS BEAUTY
Elizabeth's smooth, wrinkle-free face has turned her into an ageless queen – almost immortal in her appearance.

## CROWNING GLORY
Supported by an elaborate headdress of rubies and pearls, Elizabeth's crown affirms her status as annointed queen.

## HEAD OF STATE
High foreheads were the height of fashion in Elizabethan England and women plucked their hairlines to achieve the desired look.

## SYMBOLS OF PURITY
Elizabeth is covered in pearls of different shapes and sizes – drawing the viewer's attention to her purity and virginity. Even her cloak is lined with the gems.

## RUFF TIMES
Elizabeth wears a floating ruff that would have been set into elaborate figure-of-eight folds with the use of a special iron. By the end of Elizabeth's reign, these huge ruffs had fallen out of fashion.

## UNDER CONTROL
The jewelled serpent embroidered on Elizabeth's sleeve represents wisdom; the ruby it holds is her heart. Elizabeth, therefore, is controlled by her wisdom.

## FLOWER OF ENGLAND
The English flowers that adorn the queen's gown are reminiscent of Astraea, the celestial virgin of Classical literature who is associated with innocence and purity.

## ALL EYES AND EARS
The queen's cloak is covered with images of eyes and ears – as monarch she sees and hears everything.

# What is a quizzing glass?

There was nothing an 18th-century dandy liked more than dramatically applying a magnifying or 'quizzing' glass to one eye and directing a withering gaze at some object of disapproval. Quizzing glasses had a single lens, a handle for flourish, and were usually attached to a beaux's waistcoat or draped around a lady's neck, ready to 'quiz' the unfortunate who had just said, done or worn something outré. Although rarely *intended* to correct eyesight, they were extensions of the magnifying glass, around since the 12th century. The concept eventually became clichéd, but quizzing glasses remained popular with women until lorgnettes appeared in the 1830s, and with men until the monocle of the early 1900s.

## WHAT IS THE ORIGIN OF THE PHRASE 'WARTS AND ALL'?

At the time that Oliver Cromwell became Lord Protector of England in 1653, it was common for portraits to flatter the subject by softening or removing any blemishes. So, for Cromwell, there was no better way to distance himself from the vanity and self-indulgence of the monarchy than by having his likeness as accurate as possible.

When portrait painter Sir Peter Lely was brought before Cromwell, therefore, he was reportedly told: "I desire you would use all your skill to paint your picture truly like me ... but remark all these roughness, pimples, warts and everything as you see me. Otherwise, I will never pay a farthing for it." More than three centuries on, the phrase 'warts and all' continues to refer to anything left in its natural state.

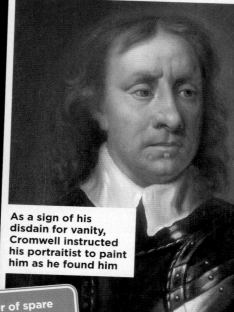

As a sign of his disdain for vanity, Cromwell instructed his portraitist to paint him as he found him

**145** The number of spare underpants (linen loincloths) found in Tutankhamun's tomb in the Valley of the Kings

# Who invented the umbrella?

The use of umbrella-like devices to provide shelter from the sun is an ancient one. Carvings from the Assyrian Empire depict parasols of circular fabric mounted on a stick as early as 1300 BC, and they appeared in China around the time of Christ. It is thought that the folding parasol, for ease of carrying, was invented in China c1270.

Although first appearing centuries earlier, parasols did not become popular in Europe until the late 16th or early 17th centuries, probably by way of visiting Persian merchants and diplomats. The word 'umbrella' was coined in Italy around 1610 to describe a particular parasol of expensive silk, decorated with gold or silver thread.

By this time, the desire for umbrellas protecting people from the rain as well as the sun was growing. In 1637, King Louis XIII of France bought the first waterproof umbrella, although sadly the name of its maker was not recorded. His umbrella had a canopy of heavy silk and was liberally soaked in thick oil to protect the monarch from Parisian downpours.

By the time the collapsible umbrella with a folding stick was developed by Marius de Paris in 1715, the umbrella had become a fashion item for ladies only. Englishmen stoically wore hats until the 19th century.

**GIMME SHELTER**
The first folding parasol was invented in 13th-century China

## WHEN WERE RIGHT AND LEFT SHOES INVENTED?

◎ **For more than 3,000 years, shoes were made by hand and with a straight profile.** Cobblers used a 'last', a foot-shaped wooden mould around which material was stretched and sewn together. These lasts were all straight until the early 1800s when American cobbler William Young designed off-centre ones, allowing him to produce footwear that better mirrored the real shape of feet. But it wasn't until the widespread adoption of machine manufacture in the 1840s and 1850s that mass-produced footwear copied the left and right pattern we now know so well.

# Why are whiskers on men's jowls called 'sideburns'?

◎ Sideburns have been cultivated for centuries – Alexander the Great is shown with them in a Pompeii mosaic – but their modern name is a tribute to the splendidly bewhiskered Ambrose Everett Burnside. Indiana-born Burnside was an inventor and politician who became a senior general in the Union Army during the American Civil War. He enjoyed some successes but was thought by many to have been promoted beyond his abilities, and is best-known for the catastrophic defeat at Fredericksburg in 1862 and his involvement in the shambolic Battle of the Crater in 1864. Burnside was an instantly recognisable figure, mostly for his distinctive style of facial hair. He grew luxuriant side whiskers joined to a moustache, sat above a clean-shaven chin. Such whiskers were soon dubbed 'burnsides' after the general and, at some point, the name was reversed to give us today's word 'sideburns'.

### DID YOU KNOW?

**GUMMY GANDHI**
Poor health caused most of Mahatma Gandhi's teeth to fall out, so – even after he had renounced personal possessions – he carried a set of dentures in his loincloth for use at mealtimes.

**BRISTLING WITH PRIDE**
General Ambrose Everett Burnside may not have been the greatest army leader but his facial hair was spectacular

# How fashion-conscious were the Vikings?

◎ The popular perception of those marauding Scandinavian invaders ignores the lengths to which they tried to keep up their appearance.

Far from being unkempt barbarians, Viking men and women actually appear to have been rather vain. Many archaeological finds – such as tweezers, combs and razors – have been discovered, offering definitive proof that they took great care when it came to personal grooming.

**TWEEZERS**
We may take the humble tweezers for granted today, but Vikings placed real value on their pluckers. This copper-alloy pair is adorned with both motifs and a glass bead.

**BONE PINS**
Delicately carved from animal bone, these pins would have been used to fasten clothing, or to secure and decorate hair.

**HAIR COMB**
Bones and antlers were carved to create hair combs and these became prized possessions. Some protective cases made especially for combs have also been uncovered.

# HOW DID THEY DO THAT?
# EASTER ISLAND

The towering statues, the moai, have stood for the last millennium – a testament to the people who made them

◎ In the middle of the Pacific Ocean is a remote patch of earth with 887 giant stone carvings – most of them stretching up four metres, but some much taller. They were sculpted by the Rapa Nui people, who first inhabited the island over 1,000 years ago. That they managed to quarry tons of volcanic rock and move the immense moai around Easter Island is a remarkable achievement.

## ISLAND STORY
### AD 300 - 800

Easter Island is settled. Legend says it was a Polynesian chief named Hotu Matu'a who arrived first with his wife and family, aboard two canoes.

## GIANTS OF STONE

Legend says that the gargantuan monolithic sculptures – the moai – could walk when commanded by a king. Now, they silently keep watch over Easter Island

**MOAI**
The reasons why they were carved are not known for sure, but it is thought that they were carved to honour and pay homage to a tribe's chiefs or deified ancestors. Most of them are cut from compressed volcanic ash, found at a great quarry called Rano Raraku on the island.

**HEIGHT**
The heights vary from four to ten metres. The height is related to the power of the clan that built it. The more powerful the clan, the taller the moai.

**AHU**
A stone platform

*4 to 10 m*

*1 to 5 m*

**PUKAO**
Some of the moai have red hat-like stones on top of the heads – red was a sacred colour.

**EYES**
Pieces of white coral with obsidian for pupils.

**HEAD**
They were positioned to face inland, facing the village of the tribe that carved them. With many moai – particularly on the slopes of Rano Raraku – their disproportionately large heads are the only thing visible, as the bodies were buried over the centuries.

## THE ISLAND

With 887 moai dotted around Easter Island, the achievements of the Rapa Nui are staggering

**AHU TAHAI**

At some sites, several moai can be seen on the same ahu – like at Ahu Tahai on the western coast.

**ANA TE PAHU CAVES**

**HANGA ROA**
Capital city of Easter island

**PUNA PAU QUARRY**

**AHU VINAPU**

Fresh water lagoon

## 1. HOW THEY WERE CARVED
Most of the giant moai were carved from rock harvested at Rano Raraku:

**1** Using stone picks, master sculptors would carve out the moai from one piece of compressed volcanic ash.

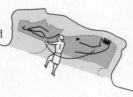

**2** The front and sides of the carving were finished before the rock underneath was chipped away, allowing it to be moved.

**3** The moai was then gradually slid down the slopes of Rano Raraku – the immense weight meant this required dozens of people.

**4** Finally, a ditch is cut at the bottom of the slope and the moai stood up inside it so the sculptor can complete the back and shoulders.

| 1200 | 1600 | 1722 | 1860s | 1888 | 1935 | TODAY |
|---|---|---|---|---|---|---|
| The Rapa Nui people are split by many tribes across the island, all of which carve moai out of volcanic rock. | Throughout the 17th century, the natural resources – especially trees – run out, and the Rapa Nui civilisation declines. | On Easter Sunday, the Dutch Admiral Jacob Roggeveen discovers the island and names it to mark the day. | Disease and slave raiders from Peru severely depletes the population. By the 1870s, only 111 people remain. | A treaty is signed by naval officer Policarpo Toro with the Rapa Nui, annexing the island for Chile. | Rapa Nui National Park is established and a mass conservation effort begins. | A third of the inhabitants work for the Chilean government, to cope with the number of tourists. |

**AHU TEPEU**

According to legend, Hotu Matu'a first landed and settled on Easter Island at Anakena. It is one of the few sandy beaches on the island's rocky coastline.

**AHU NAU NAU**

The finest example on Easter Island of the pukao, as four large moai sport their heavy red hats.

**AHU TE PITO KURA**

**TEREVAKA VOLCANO**

**RANO RARAKU**

**POIKE VOLCANO**

**AHU AKAHANGA**

**AHU VAIHU**

**EASTER ISLAND ROADS**

**AHU AKIVI**

The tomb of Hotu Matu'a, the first king and settler of Easter island.

Nearly all of the moai were made from rocks quarried at Rano Raraku.

**AHU TONGARIKI**

At Puna Pau, the red volcanic rock, scoria, was harvested for pukao.

A sacred place for the Rapa Nui – the seven moai represent the scouts sent by Hotu Matu'a to find the island.

Ancient tracks are thought to be a rudimentary road system, used to transport the heavy moai.

The largest ahu on the island, holding 15 moai – including, at over 80 tons, the heaviest moai erected.

## 2. HOW THEY WERE MOVED

Transporting the exceptionally heavy moai to their final location was a daunting task:

**1** It could take 100 people to drag a single moai, even on a wooden sledge.

**2** Using tree trunks and logs as rollers led to Easter Island being deforested.

## 3. ONTO AN AHU

Once moved, the moai were set on large stone platforms:

**1** The moai was raised by piling small stones behind it, slowly pushing it to a vertical position.

**2** The red stone pukao was added once the moai was in place.

**3** The final stage was to add the eyes, made of white coral and obsidian.

# THE TWO WORLD WARS

**DOGFIGHT DEMON**
The undisputed ace among flying aces during World War I was the splendidly named German pilot Manfred Albrecht Freiherr von Richthofen – aka the Red Baron. He had 80 combat victories to his name, 19 more than top Briton Edward Mannock.

**SPOT THE DIFFERENCE**
Monty's double (bottom right) nearly fooled German intelligence with his misleading information

# DID **MONTY** REALLY HAVE A **DOUBLE**?

Not only did Field Marshal Montgomery have a double, but the actor in the film *I Was Monty's Double* was the man who did the job! In 1939, Australian actor Clifton James joined the army, where his resemblance to Montgomery was spotted by his senior officer. James was hired by David Niven – then working for the British Army's film unit – to portray Montgomery. Instead James was snapped up by the secret service who sent him to Gibraltar and North Africa. James, pretending to be Montgomery, dropped carefully scripted comments in front of waiters, taxi drivers and others who could be relied on to blab. The comments all pointed to the Allies making their main invasion of France in the south, not in Normandy. German intelligence received the reports and – while they believed the plans for a landing were real – correctly concluded that it was merely a deception.

# What did Hitler do in World War I?

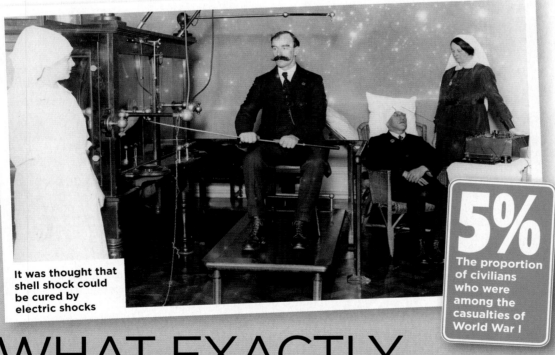

◎ The man who led Germany into World War II almost died in the first global conflict of the century. On the outbreak of war in 1914, Hitler, who had been living as an artist in Munich, signed up with the Bavarian army. He spent the next four years as a dispatch runner, delivering messages between units on the Western Front.

Hitler spent much of his time behind the front lines, but that's not to say he didn't brush with danger. He narrowly avoided death when a shell exploded next to him

**Barely recognisable, Hitler poses for the camera with his fellow soldiers during World War I**

in a trench in October 1916 and spent the following two months in hospital with shrapnel wounds to his leg. Over the course of the war, Hitler was awarded two Iron Crosses for his services.

In October 1918, Hitler found himself back in hospital after

being temporarily blinded by a British gas attack. It was while in recuperation from this that he learned Germany had lost the war. His bitterness at the news was among the many reasons that he would eventually propel Europe back into conflict in 1939.

## WHAT WAS THE FASTEST PLANE IN THE BATTLE OF BRITAIN?

◎ Although the Hawker Hurricane was the British fighter plane that claimed most victories during that key aerial battle, the more nimble Supermarine Spitfire was the speediest plane in the skies during the summer of 1940. It may not have been as effective as the Hurricane at altitudes in excess of 20,000 feet, but the Spitfire could fly 33mph faster, clocking in at a maximum speed of 362mph. The fastest German aircraft was the Messerschmitt BF 109E, which could manage a still-impressive 355mph.

---

**It was thought that shell shock could be cured by electric shocks**

## 5%
The proportion of civilians who were among the casualties of World War I

# WHAT EXACTLY WAS SHELL SHOCK?

◎ Shell shock was a term coined in 1915 to describe the psychological trauma suffered by thousands of men as a result of their experiences of the World War I.

The British Army dealt with 80,000 cases of shell shock during the war, and the condition was responsible for 220,000 men being discharged from the military as a result of disability.

Men suffering from shell shock experienced a range of symptoms – from blindness and facial tics to paralysis and vivid nightmares. Yet they couldn't expect to receive much sympathy, especially in the

war's early stages. Sufferers only received a 'wounded' category if shells had fallen nearby and many military authorities refused to define shell shock as an injury so the men could be returned to the front more rapidly.

To cure them, sufferers were subjected to primitive 'remedies' like electric shock treatment; others found themselves being accused of cowardice. In fact, the authorities' attitude to shell shock is perhaps best summed up by the extraordinary words of one British psychologist: "The frequency of shell shock in any unit is an index of its lack of discipline and loyalty."

**GENERAL GRIEVOUS**
Field Marshal Sir Douglas Haig is regarded as the most incompetent of Britain's wartime commanders

# How many horses
## died in World War I?

The success of the Steven Spielberg's 2011 film *War Horse* threw the spotlight on the role horses played in the war. As the film suggests, they suffered horribly – perhaps as many as eight million died.

At the start of the war, the cavalry was a cornerstone of the British Army, with horse-mounted units among the first to go into action against the Germans. But, as trenches, tanks and mounted machine guns came to dominate the Western Front, cavalry units increasingly found themselves banished to the sidelines.

Despite this, horses remained essential to both sides' war efforts – especially in transporting materials to the front. And the cavalry was still capable of making waves away from the Western Front – most notably in Palestine, where they played a starring role in the Allied victory over Turkish forces.

In one day during the 1916 Battle of Verdun, 7,000 horses were killed by long-range shelling. Ninety seven were killed by just one shell from a French naval gun

# WERE ANY ALLIED GENERALS IN WORLD WAR I SUCCESSFUL?

Thanks to *Blackadder Goes Forth*, it's easy to think that the Allied generals of World War I were a bunch of heartless incompetents, sending men to their deaths while sipping cocktails in a comfy château behind the lines. There certainly were some pretty dismal cases, including British general Charles Townshend, who led his troops to a quite unnecessary disaster at the siege of Kut in Mesopotamia (modern-day Iraq), and French General Nivelle's spectacularly misconceived offensive in 1917. And the record of the Italian commander General Cadorna was so bad, the Italian high command and government were all desperate to sack him. Other generals suffered major defeats, but were much more successful in later battles, like General Rawlinson, who oversaw the disastrous attack on the Somme.

But the war did produce a number of very successful generals, like Sir Herbert Plumer, who won a spectacular victory at Messines in 1917; the Canadian Sir Arthur Currie, who led the successful attack on Vimy Ridge; and the Australian Sir John Monash, who worked out a way of breaking through enemy lines without huge offensives. Meanwhile, the spectacular British victories of 1918 were the work of the most controversial military leader of all, Field Marshal Sir Douglas Haig.

**TALL ORDER**
A recruitment poster from 1915 calls for "little men" to make history

# WHAT WERE THE BANTAM BATTALIONS?

The minimum required height for British army recruits in 1914 was 5' 3", but a Member of Parliament, Arthur Bigland (yes, really), developed the idea of allowing shorter volunteers to be recruited, successfully persuading the War Office to authorise 'bantam battalions'.

The bantams – who had to be between 5' and the standard 5' 3" – proved well suited to tunnelling work, particularly the dangerous job of crawling through small spaces. Their height, however, was a disadvantage in battle. The bantams had difficulty maintaining the flow of recruits and often had to 'dilute' themselves by taking men of regulation height. When conscription was introduced in 1916, the army quietly abandoned the bantam idea and reimposed the minimum height for all new recruits.

**BANTAMS**

Little Men have made History.

**PLUCK**
CAN MAKE UP FOR INCHES.

REMEMBER

**NELSON**
AND
**ROBERTS**

Like them you can serve your Country and Help Old England in her Hour of Need.

SO JOIN THE

**BANTAM BATTALION**

Height   -   5 ft. to 5 ft. 3 ins.
Chest expanded   -   34 ins.

RECRUITING OFFICE,
THE ARMOURY, STROUD.

**GOING OVER THE TOP**
Climbing out of their trenches, troops at the Somme were cut down by machine-gun fire

# WHICH BATTLE HAD THE **HIGHEST DEATH TOLL EVER**?

◎ Modern battles can last for weeks and spread over vast amounts of territory. It is often a matter of opinion when a battle begins and ends, and where its boundaries lie. This can make it difficult to know which casualties to count, and so there are disputes over which battle cost most lives.

Operation Barbarossa, the German-led invasion of Russia in 1941, could be said to have run from 22 June to 6 December, when Russian commander General Zhukov launched a crippling counteroffensive. If so, the death toll has been estimated to have been around five million, making this easily the costliest battle ever. Other historians would say the battle ended in July when the initial German advance came to a temporary halt, giving a death toll of just under one million.

A more clearly demarcated struggle was the Battle of the Somme, which nearly every historian agrees ran from 1 July to 13 November 1916. The death toll for the Somme was around 1.2 million, making this the largest undisputed casualty figure.

The greatest death toll for a single day's combat may have occurred at Cannae in 216 BC during the 17-year-long Second Punic War. The Carthaginian general Hannibal lured a large Roman army into a trap, surrounded them on all sides and ordered a relentless massacre. Roman losses were at least 56,000 dead and perhaps as many as 92,000. Higher death tolls have been claimed at other ancient battles, but efficient Roman record keeping allows for a more accurate count to be made for Cannae than for most battles before around 1500.

**DID YOU KNOW?**

**JUST PLANE WRONG**
During the large-scale aerial skirmish on 15 September 1940, which became known as Battle of Britain Day, the RAF claimed to have shot down 185 German aircraft. However, Luftwaffe records show that only 60 failed to return.

# HOW MANY ALLIED PERSONNEL TOOK PART IN D-DAY?

◎ The invasion of Normandy by Allied troops on 6 June 1944 – D-Day – was a huge logistical challenge. The largest seaborne invasion in history, around 156,000 British, American and Canadian soldiers landed in France. Most were aboard the 7,000 vessels that crossed the English Channel, but 24,000 airborne troops landed further inland, the majority by parachute (although around 4,000 floated in aboard gliders). An estimated 2,500 Allied personnel lost their lives that day.

**6 JUNE 1944**
US 101st Airborne head for their landing position behind Utah Beach

# Why is **Walter Yeo** such an important figure in **World War I**?

◎ On 31 May 1916, Walter Yeo was manning the guns of HMS *Warspite* during the Battle of Jutland when the ship came under fire. Yeo sustained terrible facial injuries, losing both his upper and lower eyelids in the process.

In a war in which thousands of men were grievously injured, there's nothing particularly unusual in this. But what happened next makes Yeo one of the most important patients in the history of 20th century medicine. Why? Well soon after, Yeo had his face rebuilt by Dr Harold Gillies in the world's first example of modern plastic surgery.

Dr Gillies carried out his surgery on some 5,000 injured men from June 1917. Thanks to his pioneering work, thousands have benefitted from plastic surgery in the years since the war. As for Yeo, he lived until he was 70.

**Ground-breaking doctor, Harold Gillies**

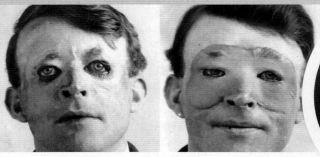

**Yeo, before (left) and after the revolutionary treatment**

**MEDAL FOR MONGRELS**
Crossbreed Rob was awarded the Dickin Medal for service including 20 parachute jumps

# WERE ANY ANIMALS DECORATED DURING WORLD WAR II?

◎ Instituted in 1943, the PSDA Dickin Medal – considered by many to be 'the animal Victoria Cross' – was awarded to 53 animals in recognition of particular gallantry, loyalty or the life-saving actions undertaken during their service in World War II.

Some 32 pigeons received the award, mostly for successfully delivering messages of crucial importance or in record time, in some cases even when injured. Eighteen dogs were decorated for their work, both on the front lines and in civil defence. The first, a mongrel called Bob, was rewarded in March 1944 for "constant devotion to duty" while serving as a patrol dog with troops in North Africa. Another, an Alsatian named Jet, was recognised for "the rescue of persons trapped under blitzed buildings" in London in January 1945. Some found themselves in the thick of battle: Rifleman Khan (another Alsatian) was decorated for rescuing an officer from drowning "under heavy shell fire" during the assault of Walcheren in the Netherlands. In 1947, three police horses received honours for calmly continuing with their duties while assisting with rescue operations in the aftermath of explosions in London between 1940 and 1944.

# 16,000
The number of British men recorded as conscientious objectors during World War I.

# WHO WAS THE LAST BRITISH SOLDIER TO DIE DURING WORLD WAR I?

◎ That unenviable record belongs to Private GE Ellison of the Fifth Royal Irish Lancers, who was shot by a unit of Germans near the Belgian city of Mons. Ellison was killed at 9.30am on 11 November 1918 – just 90 minutes before hostilities ended.

# HOW DID THE BATTLE OF THE BULGE GET ITS NAME?

◎ In December 1944, in his last major offensive of World War II, Hitler attempted to split the Allies and recapture the vital supply port of Antwerp by ordering his forces to launch a surprise thrust through the hilly and wooded Ardennes region in southern Belgium. The area was only lightly held by American troops and, caught off guard, they were initially swept aside. Within two days, some German units had advanced up to 60 miles into Allied territory, creating the 'bulge' in the frontline that gave the battle its popular name.

But their initial success was not to last, especially as they lacked the vital fuel they needed to keep their tanks and vehicles going.

As Allied resistance stiffened and improving weather allowed the Allied Air Forces to join the action, the German attack ground to a halt. In mid-January 1945, they were forced to retreat, having suffered heavy losses in men and tanks that they were unable to replace.

**ANTWERP OR BUST**
The battle was Hitler's last great play to breach Allied lines

# When were wreaths first laid at **the Cenotaph**?

The Cenotaph has been the centrepiece of services to remember the fallen since 1919. It was, at first, a wood-and-plaster structure designed by the architect Sir Edwin Luytens for the London Victory Parade of 19 July 1919, but this was pulled down soon after. Yet such was the public demand for a war memorial that Prime Minister Lloyd George and his cabinet decided to replace it with something more permanent, and again commissioned Luytens to come up with a design.

King George V unveiled Luytens' iconic Portland stone structure of an empty tomb – which is inscribed with the words 'The Glorious Dead', two wreaths and the dates of World War I – in London's Whitehall on 11 November 1920. The Cenotaph has been the site of the annual National Service of Remembrance ever since.

**The Cenotaph will soon be commemorating its centenary**

# HOW DID WORLD WAR I CHANGE **WOMEN'S LIVES**?

How much the war advanced women's rights has long been open to debate. But one fact is beyond dispute: the conflict opened up a far wider range of occupations to women than had been available to them previously.

Before 1914, many women found their job prospects restricted to domestic service. Yet, as men departed for the front, women were called upon, in their hundreds of thousands, to replace them in a wide range of workplaces.

Nearly 200,000 were employed in government departments, half a million became clerical workers in private offices, well over 100,000 worked the land, and many more worked in the munitions factories.

By 1918, the gap between male and female wages had narrowed and some women were to be given the vote. Whether that was a direct result of women's contribution to the war effort we may never know, but women's roles in society would never be the same again.

**Historian Gail Braybon claims that for many women the war was a "liberating experience", as 1.6 million entered the workforce**

## DID YOU KNOW?
### A TRULY GLOBAL CONFLICT
While the vast majority of fighting took place in Europe, more than 100 countries actively participated in World War I.

# WHAT WERE 'LITTLE BOY' AND 'FAT MAN'?

'Little Boy' was the codename for the first atomic bomb to land on Japan towards the end of World War II. Dropped by the US bomber plane Enola Gay on 6 August 1945, the 9,700lb the bomb took between 60,000 and 70,000 lives, a third of the population of Hiroshima. Three days later, the heavier 'Fat Man' bomb fell on Nagasaki, claiming an estimated further 40,000 victims. Aboard the Bockscar, the plane carrying the Nagasaki bomb, was a British airman called Leonard Cheshire. He later described the second explosion as "obscene in its greedy clawing at the earth, swelling as if with its regurgitation of all of the life that it had consumed".

# DID THE **GREAT ESCAPE** ACTUALLY HAPPEN?

Although embellished for the big screen (most notably for Steve McQueen's heroics on his motorbike), the film was actually based on a mass escape from Stalag Luft III, a German prisoner-of-war camp in Lower Silesia. Built on soft sand to deter tunnelling, the camp was believed to be escape-proof. But on a cold, moonless night in March 1944, 76 prisoners fled through a tunnel dug using cutlery and metal cans and that was secured using wooden frames fashioned from bedposts. Most were recaptured or killed, but three escaped forever.

**Air was pumped into the tunnel via a pipe made from powdered milk cans, known as 'klim' cans – 'milk' spelled backwards**

Photographed in 2007 at the age of 109, Harry Patch at the time was one of the last surviving British soldiers who saw action in WWI

# Why do we wear **red poppies** on Remembrance Day?

The story begins with the death of a young soldier, Alexis Helmer, at the second Battle of Ypres in 1915. Helmer's demise inspired his friend Lieutenant John McCrae to pen the poem *In Flanders Fields*, which references the red poppies that blanketed the fields.

McCrae's poem struck a chord with people across the combatant nations. It certainly had an impact on American professor Moina Michael. So moved was she by the lines "In Flanders fields the poppies blow/Between the crosses, row on row" that she soon launched a one-woman campaign to have the poppy adopted as the official symbol of remembrance.

The campaign was hugely successful for, by the early 1920s, poppies were being worn in France, the US and – thanks to the support of Field Marshal Haig, co-founder of the Royal British Legion – much of the British Empire. Today, the Royal British Legion produces more than 40 million poppies a year.

## WHY WAS HARRY PATCH DUBBED 'THE LAST FIGHTING TOMMY'?

When Henry John 'Harry' Patch died in July 2009 at the grand old age of 111, the horrors of trench warfare on the Western Front finally passed from living memory.

Somerset-born Patch was 18 years old when he was conscripted into the Duke of Cornwall's Light Infantry, serving as an assistant gunner. Soon after arriving at the Western Front, he was injured by a shell at the Battle of Passchendaele in 1917 and was sent home for medical treatment. He was still convalescing when the Armistice was declared.

He disappeared into obscurity until 1998 when he spoke to the BBC about his war experiences. Patch then became a bit of a celebrity, publishing an autobiography entitled *The Last Fighting Tommy*, meeting a German veteran, and speaking with great poignancy about the life on the front.

On the death of Henry Allingham on 18 July 2009, Patch became the last British survivor of the World War I trenches. He passed away seven days later.

# When was the first **two-minute silence**?

On 4 November 1919, Sir Percy Fitzpatrick, former British High Commissioner to South Africa, wrote to the war cabinet: "the hearts of our people ... desire to find some lasting expression of their feeling for those who gave their lives in the war".

Sir Percy suggested that expression could be made through a regular "three minutes' pause". The war cabinet agreed and so, with King George V's approval, set about planning a service of silence (though for two minutes instead of three) on 11 November 1919, the first anniversary of the Armistice.

When the clock struck 11am on the first Remembrance Day, Britain came to a standstill. Trams stopped running, while workers put down their tools, emptied into the streets and bowed their heads.

As the *Manchester Guardian* said the following day: "It was a silence which was almost pain ... and the spirit of memory brooded over it all."

Sombre commemorations take place on 11 November 2008, in Edinburgh

# WHEN DID WINSTON CHURCHILL FIRST USE HIS FAMOUS V-SIGN?

Initially suggested as a defiant symbol by the Belgian politician Victor de Laveleye, the BBC adopted it for their 'V for Victory' campaign that spread across Europe in early 1941. Churchill first used the gesture during a speech that July, subsequently being photographed with two fingers in the air at every given opportunity. "The V sign is the symbol of the unconquerable will of the occupied territories," he declared, "and a portent of the fate awaiting Nazi tyranny".

ALAMY X1, GETTY X6

## WHAT'S THE BEST FILM ON WORLD WAR I?

With two Academy Awards and the critics' acclaim to its name, it's hard to look past *All Quiet On The Western Front*.

Hailed by one influential movie website as "one of the most powerful anti-war statements put on film," this 1930 adaptation of Erich Maria Remarque's novel – based on his time as a German soldier on the Western Front – relates how a group of German soldiers' innocence, enthusiasm and patriotism are shattered in the trenches.

The suffering and terror are made to feel devastatingly real by director Lewis Milestone's trailblazing use of sweeping crane shots to bring the mud and blood of the battlefield to life.

Such is the respect with which *All Quiet On The Western Front* is held that in 1998 it appeared in the American Film Institute's 100 best films of the past century.

CARL LAEMMLE Presents
ALL QUIET ON THE WESTERN FRONT

*All Quiet On The Western Front* would win the Best Director Oscar in 1930 for Lewis Milestone, who had arrived in the US in 1914 with just $6 in his pocket

## How did Blackadder change the perception of World War I?

Read some newspapers and you'd be forgiven for believing that Ben Elton and Richard Curtis, writers of 1989's *Blackadder Goes Forth*, are single-handedly responsible for the modern-day view of the Western Front as an exercise in blood-soaked futility. The series charted the doomed attempts of three soldiers – Captain Edmund Blackadder (Rowan Atkinson), Private Baldrick (Tony Robinson) and Lieutenant George (Hugh Laurie) – to escape death in the trenches.

Apart from the humour, what made *Blackadder Goes Forth* so memorable was its anti-war message. Elton and Curtis conveyed this through the soldiers' relationship with their insane, bumbling commanding officer, General Melchett (Stephen Fry) – who is utterly indifferent to their suffering – and the poignant climax to the series, when the men went over the top to their certain deaths.

The show made its mark but it wasn't well received by all historians, one of whom later sniffed that the series "traded on every cliché" about the Western Front.

**Captain Blackadder and Private Baldrick on the hunt for a cunning plan**

## WHAT WAS OPERATION BARBAROSSA?

Operation Barbarossa was the German invasion of the Soviet Union, which began on 22 June 1941 and utilised in the region of four million Axis troops. By December, the Germans had advanced close to Moscow, but hadn't legislated for the brutality of the Soviet winter and a stalemate ensued – but not without combined casualties estimated at well into the millions. Hitler's aim of taking control of the Soviet Union by the end of the year had failed; he had previously boasted that "we have only to kick in the front door and the whole rotten Russian edifice will come tumbling down". And in bringing the Soviets in battle, he had fundamentally changed the direction of World War II.

# HOW DID THEY DO THAT?
# CHICHÉN ITZÁ

The awesome ruins of the Mayan city in Mexico were built to honour the skies above – and are more complex than they may at first appear

⊚ The settlement at Chichén Itzá emerged sometime in the fifth century, but really began to flourish in the 10th century. During this time, key buildings – such as the *Iglesia* (church) and the *Casa de las Monjas* (nunnery) – were constructed. The city sits near two *cenotes* – natural sinkhole wells – which were the only sources of water for the settlement.

In the 10th century, the city was invaded, possibly by the Toltecs of central Mexico. After the invasion, more advanced buildings went up, including *El Castillo*, the four-sided pyramid, and *El Caracol* (the snail) observatory. Many of the structures have an intimate link with the sun and stars - small wonder, as the Mayans had several sky gods.

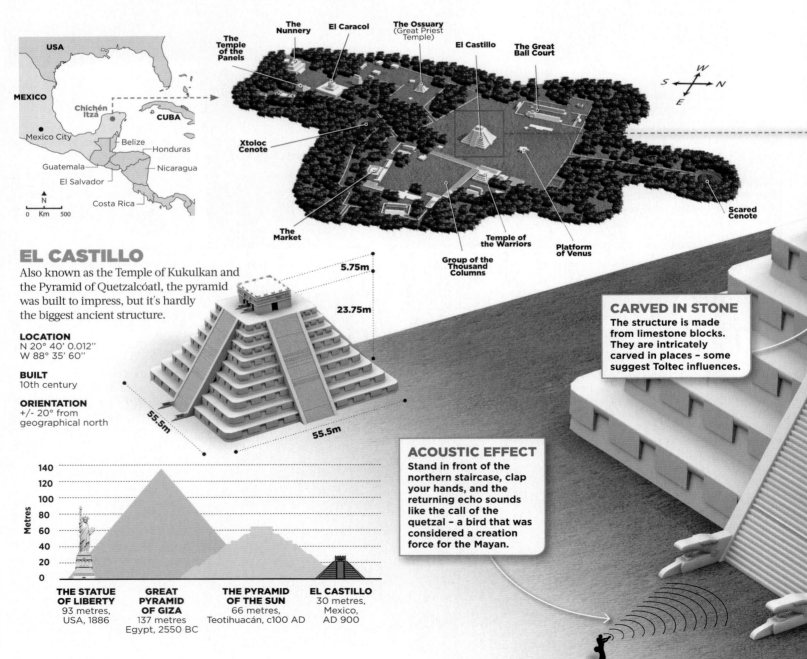

USA

MEXICO

Chichén Itzá

CUBA

Mexico City

Belize

Honduras

Guatemala

Nicaragua

El Salvador

Costa Rica

N

0    Km    500

The Temple of the Panels

The Nunnery

El Caracol

The Ossuary (Great Priest Temple)

El Castillo

The Great Ball Court

Xtoloc Cenote

The Market

Group of the Thousand Columns

Temple of the Warriors

Platform of Venus

Scared Cenote

## EL CASTILLO

Also known as the Temple of Kukulkan and the Pyramid of Quetzalcóatl, the pyramid was built to impress, but it's hardly the biggest ancient structure.

**LOCATION**
N 20° 40' 0.012''
W 88° 35' 60''

**BUILT**
10th century

**ORIENTATION**
+/- 20° from geographical north

5.75m

23.75m

55.5m

55.5m

**CARVED IN STONE**
The structure is made from limestone blocks. They are intricately carved in places – some suggest Toltec influences.

**ACOUSTIC EFFECT**
Stand in front of the northern staircase, clap your hands, and the returning echo sounds like the call of the quetzal – a bird that was considered a creation force for the Mayan.

Metres

140
120
100
80
60
40
20
0

**THE STATUE OF LIBERTY**
93 metres, USA, 1886

**GREAT PYRAMID OF GIZA**
137 metres Egypt, 2550 BC

**THE PYRAMID OF THE SUN**
66 metres, Teotihuacán, c100 AD

**EL CASTILLO**
30 metres, Mexico, AD 900

ILLUSTRATION: SOL 90

# TEMPLE OF THE RISING SUN

The Mayans were keen astronomers, as can be seen if you study the pyramid throughout the year. The Sun's movements are intrinsic to its design – the equinoxes and solstices are captured on it with remarkable precision.

**WINTER SOLSTICE**
21 or 22 December (day with least sunlight in the year)

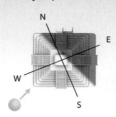

**SUMMER SOLSTICE**
20 or 21 June (day with most sunlight in the year)

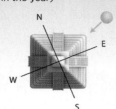

**EQUINOXES**
21 March and 23 September (days when the hours of sunlight equal the hours of darkness)

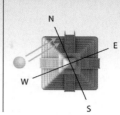

In the mid-afternoon, the combination of sunlight and shadow creates the effect of the body of a snake slithering down the stairs of the northern side of the pyramid.

## THE TEMPLE
A religious temple sits atop the pyramid. It is believed that this was the site of offerings to Kukulkan, the God that created the Universe, who appears as a feathered snake.

**SANCTUARY**

## CALENDAR CONNECTION
The pyramid has four staircases, each one with 91 steps, which add up to, together with the platform of the temple, 365 – the total number of days in a year.

**HALL**

## LAYERS OF IMPORTANCE
The pyramid is made up of nine platforms, which represent the nine levels of the Mayan underworld.

**INTERIOR PYRAMID**

15.8m

## DECORATED BOARDS

## INNER PIECE
The present pyramid lies on top of another, which was built around the ninth century.

## BASIC BEGINNINGS
Like the exterior one, this older pyramid had nine blocks and a temple, but just a single staircase on its northern side.

**FULL HOUSE**
A London classroom in 1907. School attendance was made compulsory in 1880

# WHEN DID SCHOOLING BECOME COMPULSORY?

In England and Wales, the Education Act of 1870 laid the foundations for the modern schooling system, but it was not until 1880 that law dictated compulsory education for children between the ages of five and ten years.

Unsurprisingly, this did not guarantee compliance. In reality, the required fee of 10 shillings per year – added to the fact that the child could no longer contribute to the family income – meant that poorer parents simply couldn't afford to adhere to the new legislation. It's estimated that, even after the fee was abolished in 1891, a fifth of children between these ages did not attend. Nevertheless, the British education system was gradually refined, and by 1899, the legal school leaving age had risen to 12.

# How old is the **cat flap**?

Cats were popular 9,500 years ago for their rat-catching skills and it is thought they have been domesticated for as long as 12,000 years. So it's more than probable that cat flaps are ancient. But, in Britain at least, evidence dates back to the medieval era. In Geoffrey Chaucer's *The Miller's Tale*, a character drops to his knees to peek through a door: "An hole he foond, full owe upon a bord, Ther as the cat was wont in for to crepe".

But if you want to see an old cat-hole up close, you can spot one at Chetham Library, in Manchester, built in 1421. You can also visit Exeter Cathedral, where the clock-tower was so bedevilled by mice chewing on the ropes that it possibly inspired the nursery rhyme *Hickory, Dickory, Dock, The Mouse Ran Up The Clock*. This charming tale is hard to prove, but the 17th-century cat flap in the tower door is very much real.

## £40

The amount owed to a local baker by Charles Dickens' father, John. Unable to pay, in 1824 he spent several months in a debtors' prison, forcing young Charles to work in a shoe-polish factory to feed the family.

## WHEN DID 'LONELY HEARTS' ADS START?

The earliest surviving examples date from 19 July 1695, in a publication on 'Husbandry and Trade'. Unromantically, the first advertiser states that he "would willingly Match Himself to some Good Young Gentlewoman, that has a Fortune of 3000l or thereabouts" (around £250,000 today). The second recommends himself as a 25-year-old "sober Man".

By the mid-18th century, adverts were placed by both genders. Many sought matrimony, but others were less respectable: one female advertiser offered "an advantage which cannot be named in a public newspaper" in exchange for £100.

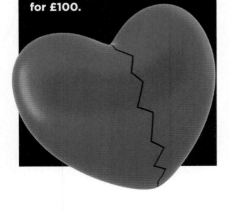

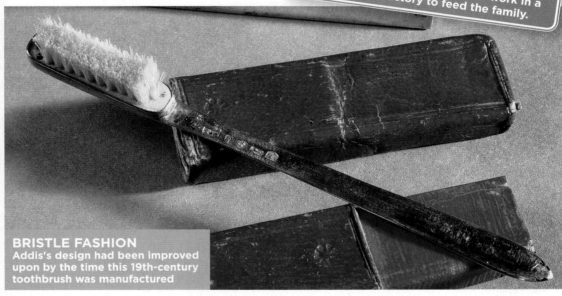

**BRISTLE FASHION**
Addis's design had been improved upon by the time this 19th-century toothbrush was manufactured

# Who invented the **toothbrush**?

The history of oral hygiene goes back a long way, with recent archaeological finds proving that there were even Stone Age dentists. But who invented the toothbrush? It depends on your definition. To freshen their breath, the people of ancient India chewed an aromatic twig, called a *dentakashta*, and the Egyptians, Babylonians, Romans and Tudors all did something similar. But it seems the first people to actually make a toothbrush were the medieval Chinese who, in the 1400s, stitched spiky pig bristles into a bamboo or bone handle. These were brought back to Europe by travelling merchants; French physicians briefly used them, but they didn't catch on in Britain. So while the Chinese can technically take all the credit, the person commonly dubbed the 'inventor' of the toothbrush is an 18th-century Brit.

William Addis was a professional rag-dealer in the East End of London. In 1780, he was chucked in Newgate Prison – perhaps for rioting – and it was here that inspiration struck.

The story goes that Addis whittled holes into a pig bone left over from his dinner and threaded them with bristles from a nearby broom, thereby creating his toothbrush prototype. When he was released from jail, he experimented with other materials and soon started selling toothbrushes. He enjoyed great success, as the sugar-obsessed population of Georgian Britain suffered appalling tooth decay.

# When did thumbs up start to mean 'OK'?

The short answer is, we can't be sure. It is widely assumed – possibly thanks to a mistranslation of Latin and its popularisation in 19th-century art – that the 'thumbs up' as a positive signal derives from the gladiatorial combats of Ancient Rome. It was used to decree that the life of a defeated gladiator should be spared.

However, an alternative theory suggests it was originally a means of signalling agreement, or sealing the deal, in medieval business transactions, accompanied with the phrase "Here's my thumb on it!". Whatever the case, the gesture was becoming commonplace by the 1600s. In *Chirologia* from 1644, John Bulwer states: "To hold up the thumbe, is the gesture ... of one shewing his assent or approbation".

## WHY DO THE VICTORIANS ALWAYS LOOK SO MISERABLE IN PHOTOGRAPHS?

**The grim-faced photographic portraits from the early days of photography colour our vision of the Victorian era, but they're not necessarily a reflection of the sitter's mood. Many no doubt intended to be captured for posterity in a pose of thoughtful contemplation or dignified authority. Yet the technology of the day (long exposure times in particular) required subjects to remain perfectly still – and a grin is difficult to maintain. It has also been suggested that, in an age of enthusiastic sugar consumption and rudimentary dental hygiene, most Victorians sitting for their portraits would have been reluctant to show their teeth.**

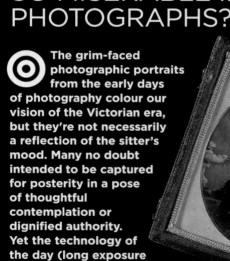

## HOW DANGEROUS WAS THE PENNY-FARTHING?

The penny-farthing was a style of bicycle popular in the 1870s and 1880s. The bike got its name from its two differently-sized wheels, with the front wheel likened to a penny coin and the much smaller rear wheel compared to a farthing (a quarter of a penny). The large wheel allowed each turn of the pedals to drive the bicycle a greater distance, and also allowed for a smoother ride over the cobbled streets and uneven roads of the period. But with the rider sitting up to 1.5 metres off the ground, broken bones were all too common in the event of accidents. Even worse, the position of the rider over the front axle meant that any sudden stop caused by hitting a stone would hurl the rider forward headfirst. Hitting the ground with the head could be, and sometimes was, fatal.

The popularity of penny-farthings waned with the development of gears, allowing the ratio between pedal and wheel to be varied. The second breakthrough was the pneumatic tyre, which gave a smoother ride. By 1893, 'safety bicycles' were on sale and penny-farthings were no longer being made.

# WHAT WAS – AND WHO FACED – **TRIAL BY ORDEAL**?

**SPLASH LANDING**
This 1920 illustration shows trial by ordeal, as endured in medieval times

How do you tell if someone is lying? In Saxon and medieval times they left it to a higher authority, and trial by ordeal was a way of working out what God's verdict was. The accused would have to plunge a hand into boiling water or walk barefoot over red-hot ploughshares. The wounds were bound up and if, after three days, they had healed, it was a sign of God's favour: not guilty.

Similar thinking lay behind throwing the accused into water, a practice common in witchcraft cases. The water would refuse an evildoer, so if you floated you were guilty; if you sank, the water embraced you because you were godly and therefore innocent. And, yes, they did fish you out!

**24** The number of offenders who could be hanged simultaneously on the infamous triangular gallows at Tyburn.

## WHO GOT THE FIRST SPEEDING TICKET?

The first person to be pulled over for exceeding the speed limit was the early car-builder Walter Arnold, of East Peckham in Kent. In 1896, he was fined a princely one shilling, plus legal costs, after being caught going at four times the speed limit! In fairness, he was only doing 8mph and suffered the curious indignity of being outpaced by a policeman on a pushbike.

The then-current law of 1865 stated that no car could exceed 4mph, and just 2mph in urban areas. The law also demanded that a pedestrian walked ahead of the car waving a red flag to alert others to the onrushing danger.

## DID PEOPLE IN TUDOR TIMES HAVE BAD TEETH?

The importance of good oral hygiene was actually well understood in Tudor times. 'Chewsticks', twigs stripped of their bark with one end split and frayed into a brush, were used on teeth and gums (and had natural abilities to combat microbes and bad breath). Nevertheless, Tudor folk did suffer tooth decay and gum disease. The instant treatment for a rotten tooth was pulling it out, so all the bad teeth in Tudor times weren't actually in people's mouths.

## WHAT WAS PIGGING?

Before modern houses were large enough for individual rooms, many poorer families often slept in the same bed. The practice was charmingly called 'pigging' and it was common in rural Scotland and Ireland right up until the 20th century. With so many snoozers crammed into a small space, a form of etiquette inevitably developed: boys and girls were kept at opposite ends while the smallest kids slept nearest their parents in the centre, creating a sort of gendered Russian doll effect. The custom possibly inspired the nursery rhyme, "There were ten in the bed, and the little one said: 'Roll over...'".

Bizarrely, though, it wasn't just family members who snuggled up under the covers. We'd be horrified if, when checking into a hotel, we found another family asleep in our room, but such renting of the family bed was common in Colonial America in the 1600s, having begun as a Dutch tradition called 'queesting'. Visiting guests, or even paying strangers, sometimes crawled in alongside mother, father and the kids to share the communal warmth. It's fair to say that if the practice were revived today, many newspaper editors would spontaneously combust from the intensity of their moral outrage!

**THREE LITTLE PIGS**
Families would often share a bed for warmth

# WHAT WAS ANGLO-SAXON LIFE LIKE?

*With Roman towns in decline, domesticity took what appears to be a step backwards*

During the post-Roman period, houses were built of less durable materials, such as timber, daub and thatch, and so are not as visible as the stone- and brick-built Roman structures that preceded them. The typical structure within both the Saxon and Celtic world appears to have been the 'longhouse', a timber hall in which both human and animal populations often shared eating, living and sleeping space.

In the west, British longhouses have been found next to malting ovens – essential for brewing beer. This implies that drinking was a significant communal activity which thrived, despite the lack of access to Mediterranean wine. *Beowulf*, a piece of English literature to survive from the period, suggests that feasting and drinking also played a major part of Saxon life. Little clothing from the time survives, but the amount of weaving finds, together with metal brooches, suggests that homemade woollen and leather items were common fashion choices.

**18**
The number of trees required to build the average Anglo-Saxon home

**LOOM IN THE ROOM**
A crucial part of Dark Ages life, weaving looms were common household items. Finds such as loom weights and spindle whorls have been found at West Stow.

## ANGLO-SAXON VILLAGE
# WEST STOW

During the Anglo-Saxon era, West Stow in modern-day Suffolk was an unassuming, largely timber-built village. At some point after the seventh century, the settlement was abandoned, but what the citizens left behind provided precious clues about daily life...

**BONE COMB**
This fragment of a sixth-century hair comb, with its ornate decoration, is carved out of bone.

**DRINKING RITUAL**
This drinking horn with silver mounts would have been used for ceremonial drinking by the elite of the early Anglo-Saxon world.

**FUNERARY VESSEL**
Cremation urns such as this were common in Anglo-Saxon communities.

**INDOOR FIRE**
Each longhouse had a simple fire, which was used for warmth, cooking and light. It was in the centre of the wooden home, which had no chimney.

**SHELF LIFE**
There was no upstairs – families and their animals slept on the ground floor – but rudimentary wall shelves were used for storage.

**"DRINKING WAS A SIGNIFICANT COMMUNAL ACTIVITY WHICH THRIVED, DESPITE THE LACK OF ACCESS TO WINE"**

**TRIPLE THATCH**
These replica thatched roofs are made of reed mix, laid over a middle layer of water reed and a base of heather. Warm and largely waterproof, they were far from long-lasting or flame-retardant.

**CENTRAL HALL**
The original settlement at West Stow was centred around a large hall – likely to be where a warrior chief or village elder would have lived. Small groups of family homes surrounded this larger hall.

**MODEL VILLAGE**
Rebuilt between the 1970s and today, West Stow village has been reconstructed using the same building **know-how, tools and materials** as the Anglo-Saxons would have had.

**SEWING TOOLS**
These pig-bone needles date from the sixth century. With such large eyes, they were used for wool, rather than fine thread.

**THE GOOD LIFE**
Re-enactors at West Stow act out the simple life of the average Anglo-Saxon

# When did people stop **attending public executions**?

◎ In past centuries, public executions of criminals had several purposes. They were a deterrent, a vengeful enactment of moral justice and a morbid form of entertainment. But in the 19th century, many Western nations began moving their gallows behind grey prison walls. Why this decision was taken is hotly debated, but it wasn't due to dwindling public interest. On the contrary, crowds in Victorian Britain were often rowdy mobs. Indeed, in 1868, the last man to be publicly executed in Britain – an Irish bomber named Michael Barrett – was booed by 2,000 people as he swung from the gallows at Newgate. For campaigners like Charles Dickens, such a furore was uncivilised and cruel, and his protests likely contributed to the change in the law.

**GALLOW'S JIG**
**Public executions were seen as a great day out for the whole family**

## HOW OLD IS THE **TOILET SEAT**?

◎ Despite the flushing toilet being a Tudor invention, pioneered by Sir John Harington (godson of Elizabeth I), the history of toilet seats goes back a long way. Communal latrines were a regular feature in Roman towns, with the bottom holes cut into the benches. These *forica* toilets are perhaps 2,000 years old, but they're positively modern compared to the limestone seats carved for posh Egyptians and Harappans (from modern Pakistan) who lived around 4,500 years ago. These seats were placed over simple drainage gullies, which could be manually flushed with water, though poorer people instead used wicker stools with a hole cut in the centre, or squatted over a ceramic pot. As for our hinged toilet seat, that was a Victorian invention more closely associated with Thomas Crapper's company.

# WERE THERE HEALTH SCARES CAUSED BY NEW TECHNOLOGY IN THE PAST?

◎ Modern newspapers often report scientific studies suggesting that children watch too much TV or that our gadgets are making us obese. But this anxious hand-wringing is nothing new. In the late 1820s, with the arrival of the passenger train, some doctors warned that speeds of 20mph would cause brain damage and the vibrations would shake people insensible. It was also suggested that herds of dairy cattle would be terrified by the noise and cause their milk to curdle in their udders. Later that century, when women took up the new hobby of cycling, a handful of (male) doctors claimed the exertion of pedalling led to ugly 'bicycle face', in which the muscles permanently froze in an unladylike gurn.

A more widely held techno-fear came from the US in the 1870s when neurologist Dr George Miller Beard claimed the pace of the modern world, accelerated by the electrical telegraph, was causing debilitating mental exhaustion. He labelled the condition *neurasthenia*. It remained a recognised medical condition for decades.

WARNING **PEDALLING WILL LEAD TO 'UGLY FACE'**

**ON YER BIKE!**
**Women were told that cycling would make them ugly**

**DID YOU KNOW?**
**ANIMAL KINGDOM**
Henry I effectively created England's first zoo in 1100 when he had a wall built to enclose his collection of exotic animals in Woodstock, Oxfordshire. A century later, the zoo was transferred to the Tower of London where it remained for the next 600 years.

# WHEN WAS TOBACCO FIRST THOUGHT TO BE DANGEROUS?

◎ The story of tobacco in Britain has always been chequered. It was initially deemed to be a medical cure for illnesses – contradicting the views of several notable people. In his 1604 treatise, *A Counterblaste to Tobacco*, King James I of England and VI of Scotland described it as "harmful to the brain, dangerous to the lungs". Soon after, the scientist Francis Bacon noted tobacco as highly addictive, while, in 1665, Samuel Pepys witnessed a cat being killed by a small dose of distilled tobacco oil. But it took another century for Dr John Hill to show that snuff tobacco could cause nose cancer, and yet another 80 years elapsed before doctors began debating the safety of smoking.

## FESTIVITIES
## AT THE THEATRE

Britain's first permanent playhouses were built during the Tudor period, but theatre's boom came during Elizabeth I's reign when works by playwrights such as William Shakespeare and Christopher Marlowe were in high demand. Companies performed 30-40 new plays every year, with all parts (including women) played by men. Playhouses such as the Globe could hold 3,000 people. A small fee would get a standing place in the pit under an open roof. The best seats were above the stage itself or in the covered gallery.

**38**
The number of plays that William Shakespeare wrote in a 27-year period

## SPORTS
## A 'BEAUTIFUL GAME'?

Football was enjoyed by all classes, but was very different to the game we know today. There was no limit to the number of players, goalposts could be as far as a mile apart, and the ball was often an inflated pig bladder. And it was dangerous. One coroner's report from the 16th century tells of two men who were accidentally stabbed while tackling an opponent.
    Bear-baiting and cock-fighting were also popular across society. Elizabeth I is known to have watched, and enjoyed, such entertainments.

**GAME AROUND**
Bear- and bull-baiting drew large crowds in the Elizabethan underworld

## IN HARMONY
## MELODY MAKERS

Music during the Elizabethan period saw a shift from sacred to secular, and musical instruments played a far greater role than previously. Bands of musicians known as waites could be found in most towns and cities. Dating back to the medieval period, waites usually played woodwind instruments, such as the shawm – a predecessor of the modern oboe.

# HOW DID TUDOR ENGLAND WORK AND PLAY?

The working day was a long one, beginning early and ending late, often six days a week. For those in work, a regular wage enabled them to feed themselves and their families, but a rapid rise in population levels during the 16th century saw thousands driven to begging on the streets. Entertainment offered ordinary Tudors respite from the daily grind – everything from football to theatre was popular.

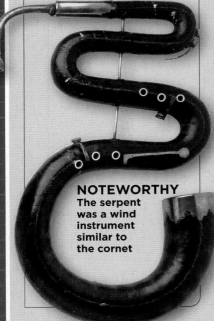

**NOTEWORTHY**
**The serpent was a wind instrument similar to the cornet**

## EMPLOYMENT
## JOBS COULD STINK

If you were lucky enough to be offered an apprenticeship at 14 years old, you could eventually earn a living as a weaver, mason, tailor or blacksmith, although you wouldn't actually qualify, or earn a proper wage, until the age of 21.
    But other Tudor jobs were not as sought after. That of the gong farmer – who cleared human waste from cesspits and privies – was surely one of the worst. Although well paid for their services, gong farmers could only work at night and were only permitted to live in outlying areas – for obvious reasons! Woad dyers had to live on the outskirts of cities: the stench created by the process used to extract blue dye from woad plants was awful.

**RAT ATTACK**
**What was top of the rubbish job chart? Possibly the rat catcher, who risked being bitten by the disease-ridden vermin**

# HOW DID THEY DO THAT?
# THE TEMPLE OF ANGKOR WAT

Cambodia's amazing architectural masterpiece was built in the 12th century and has fascinated people ever since

◎ The main construction of Angkor, the capital of the powerful Khmer Empire, Angkor Wat is masterpiece of engineering from the 12th century. The holy temple was dedicated to Vishnu, a deity in Hinduism, and is unlike anything seen before, representing a new movement in oriental art and architecture.

## THE LAYOUT

The temple is divided into three concentric enclosures that increase in height, the tallest being the central tower. During its zenith, entry to the upper levels of the temple would have been increasingly more exclusive, with the general public being admitted only to the lowest, peripheral, areas.

**STONE**
The construction required two types of sandstone: a medium grain one for the walls, and a fine grain for reliefs and decorations of the galleries.

**INTRICATE RELIEFS**
The temple has many beautiful stone carvings representing gods, as well as kings and everyday life

**LOST CITY**
Angkor Wat was once both temple and city – a vast religious building and a political centre

**ENTRANCE**
A long driveway, flanked by statues of stone, connected the entrance to the Angkor Wat site, next to the moat, with access to the monumental construction.

**FRAGILITY**
The whole ensemble was built of stone blocks piled on top of each other without mortars or arches, which helped its subsequent collapse.

# A SACRED ENCLOSURE

Angkor Wat was built in the Khmer dynasty in the reign of Suryavarman II (1113-1150). The king dedicated the temple to Vishnu as he claimed to be his incarnation on Earth.

### 1113-1145
Construction of Angkor Wat under the rule of the Khmer King Suryavarman II.

### 1177
The Khmer kingdom, weakened partly by the economic strain of Angkor Wat, is raided by the Chams. The invaders sack Angkor.

### 1181
Ascent to the throne of Jayavarman VII. Angkor Wat would be replaced as a Khmer religious centre by the new Buddhist temple of Angkor Thom.

### 1431
Thai invaders plunder Angkor, after moving the Khmer capital to the south of the country.

### 1860
French colonists bring Angkor Wat to the attention of the west and start a phase of study and reconstruction of the temple.

## GALLERIES
Each concentric square had galleries to walk through. They had stone roofs supported by pillars in a row, and the ceilings were carved to imitate tiles.

## CORNER TOWERS
These delimit the upper terrace and are shaped like lotus buds. Along with the central tower, the tops represent the peaks of Mount Meru – the abode of the gods.

TERRACE

## CENTRAL TOWER
Standing 65 metres tall, the vertex has steeped staircases, which symbolise the effort of ascension. Carved to appear like a vault, it is believed to have been undertaken as a mausoleum for King Suryavarman II.

TERRACE

## DECORATION
The walls of the colonnades that connect the main towers are decorated with beautiful reliefs.

## ICON OF A NATION
Angkor Wat has long been a crucial symbol of Cambodia's national identity, as shown in the currency of the 19th century and the current national flag.

## BALUSTRADE
The balustrade runs from the cruciform terrace at the entrance of the temple, to the central tower. It symbolizes the myth of snake of creation.

GARDEN

## BAS-RELIEFS
The outer walls are embellished with carvings illustrating the two great Hindu epics, *Ramayana* and the *Mahabharata*, along with images of Suryvarman II and scenes of everyday life at court.

**SLIP OF THE TONGUE**
A nervous Lady Diana got her royal groom's name wrong, in front of a TV audience of some 750 million viewers

# HAS THERE EVER BEEN A TRULY DISASTROUS ROYAL WEDDING?

Royal weddings rarely go without a hitch. In 1100, rumours that the bride was a runaway nun put something of a dampener on Henry I's nuptials – so much so that the Archbishop of Canterbury felt moved to deny it in the service. When the parents of the future George III wed in 1736, there were reports that the nervous bride had vomited on her new mother-in-law's skirts. Even the lavish ceremony of 1981 saw Lady Diana mixing up the groom's name with his father's.

Undeniably the most disastrous ceremony, however, was that of George, Prince of Wales and his cousin Caroline of Brunswick in April 1795. Both felt deceived by the portraits they had been sent and a reluctant George reeled into the chapel "quite drunk". After stumbling up the aisle, he barely stifled his sobs when nobody objected to the proceedings. With the ordeal over, he spent most of wedding night unconscious on the floor of their bedchamber. The marriage itself was no more successful and, by all accounts, the nuptial bed was abandoned as soon as possible.

# What happened to **King Harold's children** after he was killed at Hastings in **1066**?

⊙ William of Normandy, who became King of England after Harold's death, was not the forgiving sort. In 1066, Harold's two eldest sons, Godwin and Edmund, were in their late teens. They fled to Ireland where they lived as guests of the King of Leinster. In 1069, they came back with a fleet of ships hoping to raise an army and regain the throne. They were defeated in a battle at the River Taw in Devon. They escaped alive, but their fate is unknown.

Harold's 11-year-old daughter, Gunhilda, was being educated at Wilton Abbey in 1066. She finished her education and was married to Alan Rufus, one of William's henchmen. The marriage appears to have been happy and they had at least one child.

Gytha, who was 13, fled to her uncle, King Sweyn of Denmark, with her younger brothers Magnus, Harold and Ulf. The fates of the boys are unknown, but Gytha married Vladimir Monomakh, Prince of the Rus, and so was the ancestress to the later Tsars of Russia.

**HASTINGS IN 1066**
Harold's days were numbered, but what about his kids?

**6** The age, in days, of Mary, Queen of Scots when she became ruler of Scotland following the death of her father, James V.

**CLOAK AND SWAGGER**
There weren't enough puddles and cloaks to appease Elizabeth when Ralegh secretly married. He was sent to the Tower of London

# DID WALTER RALEGH REALLY COVER A PUDDLE FOR ELIZABETH I?

⊙ Dashing explorer and poet Walter Ralegh enjoyed the favour of Elizabeth I soon after settling at court in 1581. A testament to his gallantry and style can be seen in the well-known incident when Ralegh rescued the royal feet from getting wet and muddy in 'a plashy place' by sacrificing his plush velvet cloak to cover the puddle. Disappointingly, his cloak-laying is first recorded in Thomas Fuller's *History of the Worthies of England*, published some 80 years after the supposed event. True or not, Ralegh enchanted the queen and was one of her firm favourites – that is, until he fell from grace by secretly marrying one of her maids of honour.

# WHERE IS QUEEN BOUDICCA BURIED?

◎ Boudicca, queen of the Iceni (who lived in modern-day Norfolk), led her tribe c60 AD in a revolt against the Roman rulers of Britain. Initially successful – destroying the cities of London, Colchester and St Albans – the Iceni were finally defeated in a battle somewhere to the north-west of London. Roman sources suggest the slaughter of around 200,000 Britons.

The exact location of the battle is unknown, although Lewis Spence, in his 1937 book *Boadicea - Warrior Queen of the Britons*, suggested, with no real evidence, that the opposing armies had fought on land now occupied by the railway stations of King's Cross and St Pancras. The Roman historian Dio Cassius, writing over a century after the battle, suggested that, in defeat, Boudicca "fell ill and died", her followers providing her with a lavish burial. In truth, this seems unlikely, given that reprisals followed in the aftermath of the revolt, and Dio Cassius provides no source for the claim.

This hasn't prevented people searching for a grave, however, and the myth that her last resting place today lies somewhere beneath platforms 9 and 10 of King's Cross seems to be more popular than ever, probably thanks to Spence's book. The story appears to have inspired the author JK Rowling, who placed the departure point of the Hogwarts Express – which takes Harry Potter and his classmates to their school of witchcraft and wizardry – at King's Cross platform 9¾.

**LAST STOP**
Could the tribal queen be buried beneath so regal a place as King's Cross Station?

## 60
The number of maids of honour in the court of Queen Anne Boleyn.

# WHICH ROSE WON THE WAR?

◎ **The Wars of the Roses ended at the Battle of Bosworth in 1485 but, technically, neither side won.**

The wars had nothing to do with the counties of Yorkshire and Lancashire, but was a dispute between rival branches of the family of Edward III. On one side were supporters of Duke of Lancaster John of Gaunt, while on the other was Edmund, Duke of York. As Henry Tudor's victory over Richard III marked the end of the Plantagenets, neither the red nor white rose was the clear victor, despite Henry's distant connection to Lancaster.

# DID HENRY VIII HAVE ANY ILLEGITIMATE MALE OFFSPRING?

◎ Notoriously male-child light, Henry VIII must have been frustrated by the fact he was able to father boys out of wedlock with comparative ease. There are rumours that the King sired seven children, including five boys.

Henry, however, only officially acknowledged one. Henry Fitzroy was the son of Elizabeth 'Bessie' Blount, one of Catherine of Aragon's ladies in waiting (the prefix 'Fitz' refers to illegitimate offspring while 'roy' is an anglicised version of 'roi', meaning 'king'). His exact birthdate is unknown as it was, for obvious reasons, hushed up, but it was sometime around June 1519. Six years later, as it became increasingly clear the king was having problems in the heir-department, Henry suddenly acknowledged young Fitzroy.

In an elaborate ceremony, Henry showered money and honours upon his son, including a double-dukedom (Richmond and Somerset). Suggestions that the new duke should be married to his older half-sister, Mary – thus shoehorning him to pole-position for the throne – came to nothing. Any other cunning plans about his succession ended with Fitzroy's early death in 1536, more than ten years before his father's demise.

**BAD HEIR DAY**
Henry Fitzroy was the son Henry craved, but never got to be king

**SECRET WEDDING?** Rumours surround the marriage venue of Henry VIII and Jane Seymour

# Where did **Henry VIII** marry **Jane Seymour**?

Henry VIII was betrothed to Jane Seymour on 20 May 1536, just one day after the execution of her predecessor, Anne Boleyn. Jane became his third wife ten days later, in a private ceremony at 'the Queen's Closet' at Whitehall Palace, London (then also known as York Place). But whispers of other secret ceremonies gradually developed into traditions. By the 1820s, it was established in local folklore that Jane had in fact been 'wooed and wed' at Marwell Hall, Hampshire, the property of her brother Henry; the alleged chamber was even pointed out to visitors. Other 19th-century sources bestow the honour on her father's home at Wolfhall, Wiltshire. Another theory, perhaps based on an ambiguous phrase in a courtier's letter, sets it in nearby Tottenham Parish Church.

There is no way of confirming whether a secret ceremony was conducted elsewhere, but the lack of contemporary evidence makes it unlikely. Whatever the case, Henry was to be delighted with his choice of wife – the motto she chose was "bound to obey and serve".

## DID QUEEN VICTORIA HAVE A CHILDHOOD NICKNAME?

Victoria's childhood was miserable. The 'Kensington System', adhered to by members of the royal family, restricted the princess's privacy and confined her to the palace. This was all part of a controlling strategy enacted by her overbearing German mother, Victoria, and her guardian, Sir John Conroy. Young Victoria was their ticket to power, but they didn't call her Victoria – this was her second name. In fact, her baptismal name was Alexandrina, in honour of her godfather, Tsar Alexander of Russia, and so, to them, the little princess was simply 'Drina'.

## HOW MANY ENGLISH KINGS HAVE BEEN CALLED HENRY?

Henry VIII was the last king to bear that name – but he was actually the ninth. Henry II, who reigned between 1154-89, had grown up in France, where royal apprenticeships were customary. Hence, in 1170, he decided that his eldest son would be crowned as Henry the Young King – a junior co-monarch – to learn the art of kingship. Young Henry died before his father and, despite being crowned, never took the title Henry III. That title instead went to the son of King John.

# WHY DID CHARLES II TAKE OUT AN ADVERT IN THE PAPER?

In June 1660, a plea for information, written by the king himself, appeared in the *Mercurius Publicus* newspaper, stating: "We must call upon you again for a Black Dog between a greyhound and a spaniel...It is His Majesties own Dog, and doubtless was stolen, for the dog was not born nor bred in England, and would never forsake His master... Will they never leave robbing his Majesty! Must he not keep a Dog?" One of Charles's courtiers wasn't so keen on the king's pooches: "God save Your Majesty, but God damn your dogs!"

**BLING SPRING**
The fountain combined two of Henry's loves: wine and showing off

**WHAT'S IN A NAME?**
Prince Albert's marriage to Queen Victoria brought multiple hyphens to the British monarchy

# WHO WERE THE SAXE-COBURG-GOTHAS?

◎ Until the 1870s, the realm we now call Germany comprised dozens of mini-states. In Saxony, the lands of dead nobles were split between brothers, rather than simply being inherited by the firstborn. Resulting territories included the large Grand Duchy of Saxe-Weimar-Eisenach, plus the smaller duchies of Saxe-Gotha-Altenburg, Saxe-Meiningen, Saxe-Hildburghausen and Saxe-Coburg-Saalfeld.

Prince Albert, the most famous member of the House of Saxe-Coburg-Gotha, was born a Saxe-Coburg-Saalfeld. His great-uncle's death in 1825 led to a baffling swapping of lands, creating four large Saxon states. When Gotha-Altenberg became an extinct line, Gotha was exchanged for Saalfeld. So when Prince Albert married Queen Victoria in 1840, Saxe-Coburg-Gotha became the house of the British monarchy.

## WHAT WINE WAS SERVED IN HENRY VIII'S WINE FOUNTAIN?

◎ Henry VIII adored novelty, bling and dispensing his largesse – and a gigantic golden fountain that flowed wine instead of water ticked all his boxes. The famous painting of Henry's meeting with the French King Francis I at the Field of the Cloth of Gold shows such a fountain in full flourish.

When archaeologists uncovered the remains of a 16th-century fountain at Hampton Court Palace, they just had to recreate it. Four metres high and made of timber, lead, bronze and gold leaf, it now pours wine daily for palace visitors. Perhaps a little 'vulgar' to modern eyes, Tudor guests would have been dazzled by the gilded glamour on display.

In the days before bottling and corks, wine would have been drunk young, before it had a chance to 'go off'. Brought from France in barrels, it would have tasted very 'new' to us, not unlike Beaujolais Nouveau.

**DID YOU KNOW?**
**HRH ALPHONSO**
Had he lived to succeed his father and not died in 1284, the next king of England after Edward I would have been called Alphonso.

**13** The age of Margaret Beaufort, Henry VII's mother, when she was widowed in 1456. She was seven months pregnant with Henry and it was her second marriage – the first was annulled as she was a toddler at the time.

# Which king of England was the most lecherous?

◎ There are quite a few claimants to this title. Although Henry I had only one legitimate son, he did manage to father more than 20 illegitimate children with a variety of mistresses. Charles II's mistresses – and the 14 children he had with them – are well-documented, while according to medieval chroniclers, King John was forever seeking to seduce the wives and daughters of his barons.

However, England's most lecherous monarch may well have been Edward IV. According to an Italian at his court "he was licentious in the extreme... He pursued with no discrimination the married and unmarried, the noble and the lowly."

The least lecherous? This was almost certainly Henry VI, the king he overthrew. It was said that when a nobleman provided topless dancers at a dinner for him, the young king averted his eyes and fled the room.

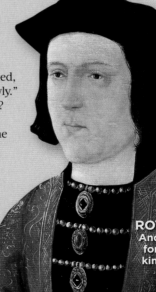

**ROYAL LINE**
And the award for raunchiest king goes to...

# WHAT HAPPENED AT THE EXECUTION OF CHARLES I?

On 30 January 1649, after saying goodbye to his youngest children and putting on an extra shirt in case he shivered in the cold – which his enemies may mistake for trembling in fear – Charles stepped out onto a black-draped wooden scaffold outside the Banqueting House at Whitehall. Nobody had been able to find the usual execution block and so a lower one, usually used for dismembering traitors, was there in its place. Unable to address the crowd from a raised platform, he spoke to those around him, justifying his actions. He then laid his head upon the block, stretched out his arms to indicate he was ready and the unknown executioner cut off his head with a single blow. The watching crowd greeted the moment with a loud groan of dismay. Concerned that his grave might become a place of pilgrimage, the new regime had his body buried at Windsor inside the castle walls in St George's Chapel.

**ALL THAT REMAINS**
RIGHT: **Today, a bust of Charles I looks down on the site of his beheading**
FAR RIGHT: **The silk vest worn by Charles during his execution**
BELOW: **Charles's death warrant. Cromwell's signature is third down in the left-hand column**

# HOW DID THEY DO THAT?
# SAINT BASIL'S CATHEDRAL

## The eye-catching masterpiece of Moscow incorporates ten churches in one dazzling domed confection

The Cathedral of the Intercession of the Most Holy Theotokos on the Moat, more commonly known as the Cathedral of Vasily (Basil) the Blessed, is a kaleidoscopic creation of red-brick towers and striped onion domes. Originally comprising eight separate churches surrounding a central church of intercession – the tenth was added later – each of its components commemorates an event, is devoted to different saints and boasts its own treasures. Reaching to the sky like the flames of a giant bonfire, it's quite unlike any other building in Russia – or, indeed, anywhere else. It was confiscated by the Soviet state in 1928 and is now a museum.

## THE SYMBOLISM OF DOMES

The origin of 'onion' domes in Russia is debated. Some think they were first used in Novgorod around 1050, while others believe that Ivan the Terrible introduced them in the 16th century. The symbolism is also debated. It's said that the form is designed to resemble a candle (Jesus being the 'light of the world'). A single dome represents Jesus; three, the Holy Trinity; five, Christ and the four evangelists; 13, the saviour and 12 apostles. Colours are also significant: gold symbolises Jesus; blue the Holy Spirit or Virgin Mary; green the Holy Trinity.

## TOWERS OF THE TERRIBLE

Built by Tsar Ivan IV ('the Terrible') between 1555 and 1561 on the site of a Trinity Church, St Basil's commemorates Ivan's earlier conquest of Kazan. The cathedral's towers may originally have been topped with 'helmet' domes that were replaced by the 'onion' style later that century. Added to and restored several times, the cathedral is believed to have been designed by two architects, Barma and Postnik Yakovlev. Ivan ordered they be blinded after the cathedral's completion to ensure that they could never build anything else to compare with it – or so legend has it.

**KREMLIN CONFUSION**
Towering over Moscow's Red Square, St Basil's Cathedral is often mistaken for the Kremlin

**TERRIBLE TSAR**
Ivan IV may have been mentally unstable and was feared for his brutal policies

**CHURCH OF SAINTS CYPRIAN AND JUSTINIA**
This church is devoted to fourth-century martyrs from Antioch, beheaded by order of the Roman Emperor Diocletian.

**CHURCH OF THE ALEXANDRIA PATRIARCHS**
Dedicated to Saints Alexander, John and Paul.

**CHURCH OF SAINT ALEXANDER SVIRSKY**
Dedicated to a monk who was canonised less than ten years before St Basil's was built.

**CENTRAL TOWER**
Though from the west front the church appears symmetrical, the central tower is actually slightly offset to allow room for the nave at the east.

**BELL TOWER**
In the 17th century, a hip-roofed bell tower (not shown) was added at the south-east of the main complex.

**CHURCH OF THE INTERCESSION**
At 46 metres high, the tented tower of the central church soars high above the complex.

**CHURCH OF THE ICON OF SAINT NICHOLAS THE MIRACLE-MAKER**
At 28 metres tall, this church is one of the largest of the complex. It's named for a famous icon miraculously found in a forest by the Velikaya River.

**GOD'S GOLD**
The interiors of the ten churches at St Basil's are lavishly adorned with colourful decoration

**CHURCH OF THE HOLY TRINITY**
Built on the site of the original church, which was in a busy market area.

**CHURCH OF THE ENTRY OF CHRIST INTO JERUSALEM**
This church preserves various relics from the past, including a projectile that hit the building during the revolution of October 1917.

**CHURCH OF SAINT BARLAAM OF KHUTYN**
Dedicated to a 12th-century Russian hermit.

**CHURCH OF SAINT GREGORY THE ILLUMINATOR**
Dedicated to the saint who, in AD 301, converted Armenia to Christianity.

**CHURCH OF SAINT BASIL THE BLESSED**
This small temple, added in 1588, is dedicated to the saint who died in 1552 and whose name was later adopted for the whole cathedral.

**WHITE STONE FOUNDATIONS**

**BLACK GOLD**
Edward, the Black Prince, is buried at Canterbury Cathedral

**DID YOU KNOW?**

**TOE-CURLING FASHION**
In Medieval times, fashionable men wore long, pointed shoes with padding in them to show how virile they were. To avoid tripping on them, some curled up the ends and tied them to their legs.

# HOW DID THE BLACK PRINCE GET HIS NAME?

Edward Plantagenet, eldest son and heir of England's King Edward III, was known during his lifetime as Edward of Woodstock, after his birthplace. The sobriquet 'Black Prince' does not appear in written records until the 16th century, nearly two centuries after his death, although as a nickname it may date back to his lifetime.

The origin of the term is just as obscure as the date it was first used. It may stem from Edward's habit, when jousting, of putting aside his royal coat of arms in favour of a black 'shield for peace' decorated with three white ostrich feathers. Some historians believe he also wore black armour, while others have suggested that the name may have been derived from the French habit of referring to a particularly brutal commander as a 'black boar'. In truth, we do not know for certain.

# Why was the Spanish Inquisition so terrifying?

◎ In 1478, Ferdinand of Aragon and Isabella of Castile asked the Pope for an inquisition to see if Jewish and Muslim converts to Catholicism in Spain were secretly practising their original faith. This Spanish Inquisition also sometimes investigated Protestants, who retaliated with a lurid propaganda campaign, with stories of fiendish torture chambers and thousands put to their deaths.

The truth is much more boring. The Inquisition were canon lawyers who spent their time on paperwork. They seldom used torture, precisely because they knew evidence extracted under torture is unreliable. They usually dismissed witchcraft cases for lack of evidence. They did, though, burn people at the stake – the usual punishment for religious offences – but they never had the political power their enemies imagined.

**FIRE & PUNISHMENT**
Not sticking to Catholicism? The Inquisition could have you burned at the stake

## WHAT WAS THE 'KING'S EVIL'?

◎ People in medieval England and France suffered from scrofula, a disease of the lymph glands, which was called the King's Evil. It was thought to be cured by the touch of a monarch. Most royals did nothing to dissuade this idea as it underlined the divine nature of their rule. The first ceremonial touching goes back to the reign of either Henry III or Edward I. By the 15th century, events were being organised so monarchs could touch hundreds of diseased people. Henry IV of France touched no fewer than 1,500 people.

# Could medieval criminals really claim sanctuary in churches?

◎ Yes. The concept that you could avoid prosecution by getting to a sacred place was accepted in England well before the Norman Conquest. Some churches had special knockers (such as Durham Cathedral, pictured here), which a fugitive had only to touch to be safe. Sometimes, like at Beverley in the East Riding of Yorkshire, the right of sanctuary extended beyond the church to a safe area often marked by stone crosses.

Some sites offered permanent sanctuary, but normally a person had 40 days in which either to stand trial or leave the country. If they refused both, they could be starved into submission. If they chose the second option, they were given a special outfit to wear and a staff or cross to carry, and told to make for a particular port.

In 1486, it was ruled that sanctuary did not apply to cases of treason. This was bad news for Humphrey Stafford, who had been hauled out of sanctuary in Culham Church in Oxfordshire after rebelling against Henry VII – he was hanged, drawn and quartered. Shortly after this, Pope Innocent VIII declared that second offenders could not claim sanctuary. Both Henry VIII and James I further limited the right of sanctuary, and it finally disappeared totally in the 18th century.

**HANDLE OF GOD**
Just a touch of this knocker would protect fugitives from the law

# WHAT WERE THE ELEANOR CROSSES?

When Edward I's wife, Eleanor of Castile, died near Lincoln in November 1290, the grief-stricken king gave orders for her body to be brought back to Westminster for burial. The journey took 12 days and Edward decreed that a stone monument should be erected to mark each of the places where her coffin rested for the night en route. Though they're called crosses, they were in fact pointed monuments incorporating heraldry and statues of the late queen. Of the original monuments built, three still survive – at Geddington and Hardingstone, both in Northamptonshire, and at Waltham Cross in Hertfordshire.

**CROSS PURPOSES**
Twelve Eleanor Crosses were constructed to commemorate Edward I's queen

## 100 million
The highest estimate of Black Death casualties during the 14th century

# WHAT WAS THE BALL OF THE BURNING MEN?

In an unlikely sequence of events, what began as a joyful royal celebration in medieval France ended in a tragedy that claimed the lives of four people.

On 28 January 1393, a masquerade ball was held at the French royal court to celebrate the marriage of one of the Queen's ladies-in-waiting. The young King Charles VI and five of his noble companions performed a dance as 'wild men', disguised in masks and shaggy costumes made from linen and resin.

Late, and somewhat intoxicated, the Duke of Orleans arrived carrying a lit torch, being unaware of the strict prohibitions on bringing naked flames into the hall. One account describes how he then 'threw' the torch at the dancers, but others suggest he simply came too close to them while trying to guess their identities. Whatever the case, the dancers' highly flammable costumes soon became engulfed in flames. The King, standing a little apart, was saved when his teenage aunt threw her skirts over him to put out the fire. Another dancer leaped into a vat of wine.

The other four performers were less fortunate, being "burned alive" and "releasing a stream of blood". The tragedy shook public confidence in the monarchy – destroying the reputation of the Duke of Orleans, in particular – and became known as the 'Bal des Ardents', or the 'Ball of the Burning Men'.

**FLAMING HELL**
Four dancers burned to death at a French masquerade ball

# HAS THERE EVER BEEN AN ENGLISH POPE?

Just one – Nicholas Breakspear, who became Pope Adrian IV in 1154. Breakspear was born around 1100 in humble circumstances at Abbots Langley in Hertfordshire, but didn't spend much of his life in England. He studied in Paris, then joined the Abbey of St Rufus in Provence, where he was elected abbot. He seems to have been able and hardworking. Made cardinal by Pope Eugenius III, he was sent to Scandinavia to reorganise the church there. After that success, he was elected Pope after Eugenius' successor, Anastasius IV, died, taking the name Adrian IV.

It was a difficult time to be Pope. Adrian had to deal with revolts in Rome, problems with the Normans in the south of Italy, and a quarrel with the Holy Roman Emperor, Frederick Barbarossa. He is rather a controversial figure in the history of the British Isles because he also apparently gave King Henry II of England papal approval for the conquest of Ireland. He died in 1159.

**BRIT POPE**
Adrian IV, formerly known as Nicholas Breakspear

## WHY DID PLAGUE DOCTORS WEAR BEAKED MASKS?

With a long cloak and grotesque bird-like mask, the plague doctor was far from a comforting sight. The first description of such an outfit dates back to 1619, from a physician of the Medicis, Charles de Lorme: "The nose [is] half a foot long, shaped like a beak, filled with perfume". The hooked snout contained substances thought to ward off the pestilence in the bad air, including lavender, camphor, vinegar sponge or laudanum.

# When did the **Tower of Pisa** start to lean?

Begun in 1173, only the third storey was complete when the foundations shifted, tilting the white marble bell tower northwards. To correct the lean, builders elongated the fourth-storey pillars on the north side, but building was stopped until 1272 when Pisa was dragged into a century of warfare. By then, major subsidence had wobbled the masonry towards the south instead. Although completed, Pisa's tower has remained in an unwinnable battle against the ever-shifting soil.

### DID YOU KNOW?

**HRH ALPHONSO**
Had he lived to succeed his father and not died in 1284 at the age of ten, the next king of England after Edward I would have been called Alphonso.

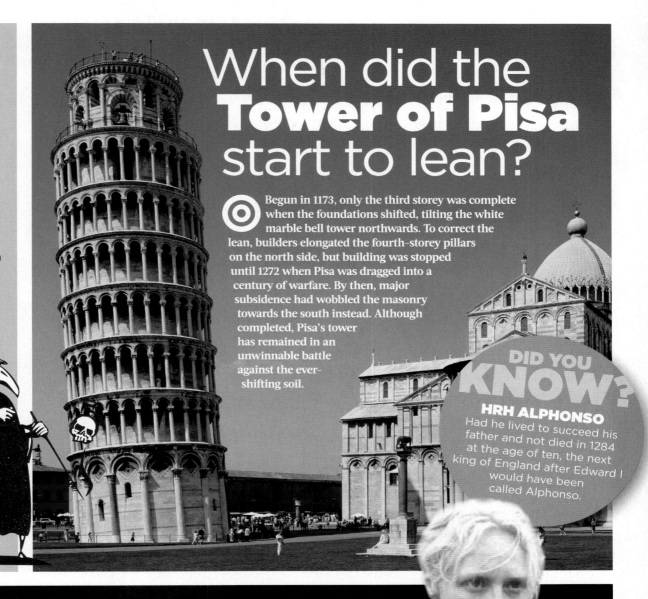

# Could a **woman become a knight** in medieval times?

A medieval knight had a number of set roles and duties – not least to fight in battle and lead men to war. As a result, it was usual for knights to be men who had trained for warfare from an early age. However, the situation wasn't quite so clear-cut.

Any man who held enough land to afford the cost of arms and armour, and to take time away from his estates to join the army, was expected to be a knight. He would have to turn up at any military muster, mounted and armed, and very often would bring a retinue of men at arms or archers. The king also expected knights to maintain law and order, ensure taxes were paid, and keep roads repaired and river crossings usable.

When a dead knight's land passed to his wife or daughter, these duties were imposed on that woman. In England, the title of Lady was usually given to such a woman but, in France, Tuscany and Romagna, she was given the male title. In 1358, women finally gained full knightly acceptance in England when they began to be admitted to chivalric orders – though they are called dames, not knights.

**CHAIN MALE**
Women inherited knightly duties – though not fighting

**WARNING: NOT FOR THE FAINT HEARTED**

# What were the worst medieval torture methods?

## THE IRON MAIDEN

The mere sight of this huge upright coffin – which supposedly dates back to the Middle Ages – strikes fear into the eyes of its beholder. But only those unfortunate enough to end up inside know its true horror. Lined with strategically placed spikes to penetrate the victim's most sensitive parts – but, crucially, to avoid the vital organs – the doors are slowly shut. Death follows even more slowly, as the Maiden can take days to claim its victim.

## THE WHEEL

If used creatively by Middle Ages torturers, the wheel was a deadly tool. Basic methods include burning a person's various parts as they are rotated around, while possibly the cruellest use was more of a crucifixion. The prisoner's limbs were broken, shoved in between the wheel's spokes, then they were raised to the top of a pole for days.

## SCAVENGER'S DAUGHTER

Designed to crush the body, this device could crack bones, dislocate the spine, and force blood out from the ears and nose. Forced to crouch down, the victim's neck would be placed in the top of the instrument, the wrists encased in the hoops at the middle, and the ankles locked into the bottom. With a twist of a screw, the torturer tightens the device, squeezing the victim, little by little, to death.

## THE RACK

Often considered the most painful torture of them all, a stretch on the rack left you more than a little loftier. It would dislocate limbs with a loud crack – and an overzealous torturer could even rip off arms. Although designed for extracting information, this device did often kill – or, at best, left you crippled.

## THE HERETIC FORK

This nasty instrument was reserved for heretics. After a confession, the collar is wrapped around the neck, with the fork prongs sinking their way into the chest at one end and the chin at the other. The head is forced up and back, causing extreme discomfort, and the dissenter is often thrown in jail while subjected to the torture.

## HEAD CRUSHER

Supposedly a favourite of the Spanish Inquisition, this contraption does exactly what its name suggests. With the prisoner's chin placed on the bottom plank, a turn of the crank crushes the cranium. In some instances, death comes only after the victim's teeth have broken from the pressure and the eyeballs have popped out of their sockets.

## BREAST RIPPER

If a woman was suspected of having an abortion or of committing adultery, she might find herself on the wrong end of these prongs. After inserting the forks – sometimes hot from the fire – into the breasts, the torturer rips the bosoms apart. If the prisoner survives the pain and blood loss, her chest is left mutilated.

## SAW TORTURE

Simple but effective, saw torture could be conducted without any specialist equipment and was dished out as a punishment for all sorts – witchcraft, blasphemy and theft, to name but a few. But its simplicity should not be underestimated. The victim is hung upside down so as to slow blood flow to the sliced area, and also to keep blood in the head, thus maximising consciousness and pain, and prolonging death.

## THE BRAZEN BULL

Invented in Ancient Greece, medieval torturers were fans of this cruel apparatus. The condemned is placed inside a hollow metal bull and a fire is ignited beneath – essentially burning the person alive. For any witnesses, the muffled deathly screams sound more like a cow, the dying prisoner's movements make the bull twist and turn, and all the steam and smoke within is funnelled out through the ox's nostrils. It really does look like a brazen bull.

## JUDAS CRADLE

Being impaled on this pointed 'seat' for days may not kill a person, but infection would – the device was rarely cleaned. Some torturers hang weights off their victims' legs, while others oil the point to push up the pain.

# HOW DID THEY DO THAT?
# ACROPOLIS

## Athens' greatest monument is a symbol of civilisation

◎ *Acropolis* translates as 'topmost city': a citadel on a high place. But the Acropolis of Athens, which largely dates back to the fifth century BC when Pericles was leader of the city, is more than merely a collection of old buildings on a craggy outcrop. This depiction, recreating the sacred precinct in its heyday, shows why it is described by UNESCO as "the site of four of the greatest masterpieces of classical Greek art ... symbolising the idea of world heritage".

## PORCH OF THE CARYATIDS

The roof of the Erechtheion's south porch is supported by six Caryatids – statues of the maidens of Karyes who danced in honour of the goddess Artemis.

### CLASSICAL GREECE

Thebes
Corinth ● ●ATHENS

### ATHENS

● Eleusis
*Kifissos River*
*Gulf of Eleusina*
ACROPOLIS 🏛
*Ilisos River*

## STATUE OF ATHENA PROMACHOS

Only chunks of the marble base of this 9m-high bronze statue remain. It was sculpted by Phidias around 456 BC and displayed spoils from the victory over the Persians at Marathon.

## ERECHTHEION

This elegant temple, erected 421-406 BC, was named for a mythical king of Athens and housed altars of several cults including those of Poseidon and Athena Polias.

IONIC COLUMNS

## THE FRIEZE

An epic frieze – a marble relief depicting a mass procession – extended 160m around the *cella* (walled inner structure). Most of the surviving 130m is in the British Museum in London.

33.6m

## PROPYLAEA

This monumental marble gateway – the main entrance to the Acropolis – was built 437-432 BC.

## BEULÉ GATE

Named after a 19th-century French archaeologist, this narrow defensive entrance was added around AD 280.

## TEMPLE OF ATHENA NIKE

Built around 426-421 BC after the destruction of an earlier wooden temple in 480 BC, this later Ionic structure was also demolished by the Turks in 1686 and its stone used for building. It was rebuilt in 1835.

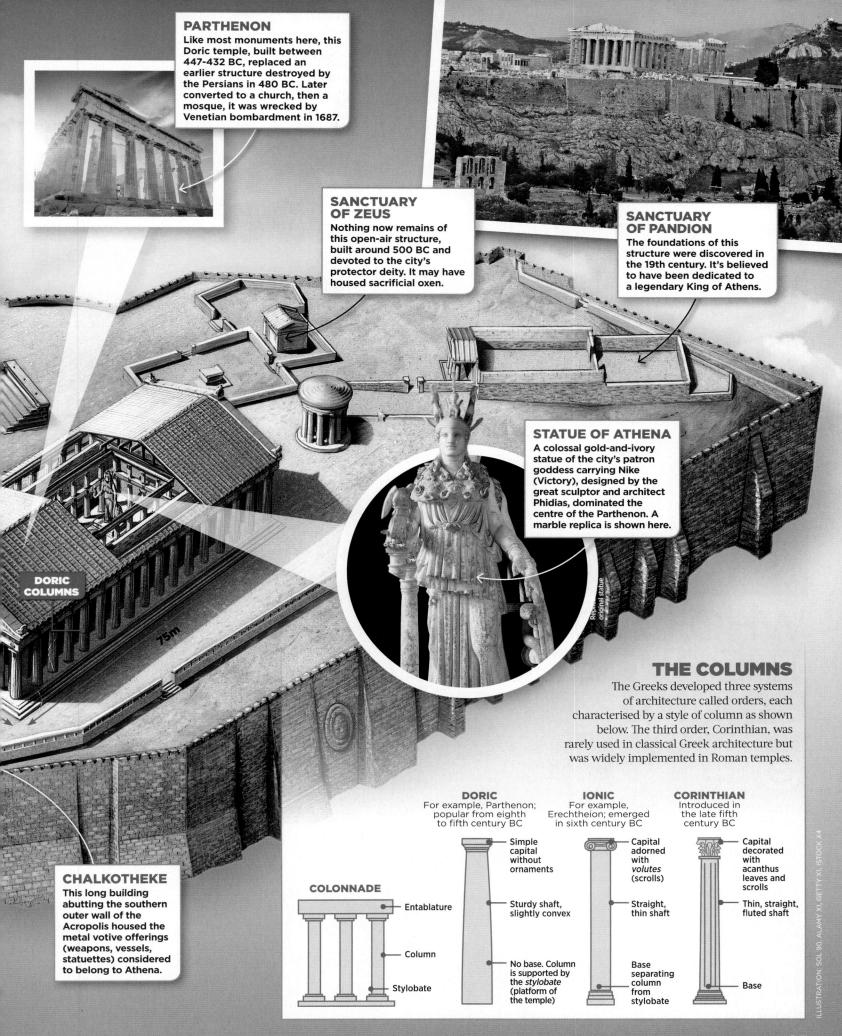

**PARTHENON**
Like most monuments here, this Doric temple, built between 447-432 BC, replaced an earlier structure destroyed by the Persians in 480 BC. Later converted to a church, then a mosque, it was wrecked by Venetian bombardment in 1687.

**SANCTUARY OF ZEUS**
Nothing now remains of this open-air structure, built around 500 BC and devoted to the city's protector deity. It may have housed sacrificial oxen.

**SANCTUARY OF PANDION**
The foundations of this structure were discovered in the 19th century. It's believed to have been dedicated to a legendary King of Athens.

**STATUE OF ATHENA**
A colossal gold-and-ivory statue of the city's patron goddess carrying Nike (Victory), designed by the great sculptor and architect Phidias, dominated the centre of the Parthenon. A marble replica is shown here.

Replica of
original statue

DORIC
COLUMNS

75m

**CHALKOTHEKE**
This long building abutting the southern outer wall of the Acropolis housed the metal votive offerings (weapons, vessels, statuettes) considered to belong to Athena.

## THE COLUMNS
The Greeks developed three systems of architecture called orders, each characterised by a style of column as shown below. The third order, Corinthian, was rarely used in classical Greek architecture but was widely implemented in Roman temples.

**COLONNADE**
- Entablature
- Column
- Stylobate

**DORIC**
For example, Parthenon; popular from eighth to fifth century BC
- Simple capital without ornaments
- Sturdy shaft, slightly convex
- No base. Column is supported by the *stylobate* (platform of the temple)

**IONIC**
For example, Erechtheion; emerged in sixth century BC
- Capital adorned with *volutes* (scrolls)
- Straight, thin shaft
- Base separating column from stylobate

**CORINTHIAN**
Introduced in the late fifth century BC
- Capital decorated with acanthus leaves and scrolls
- Thin, straight, fluted shaft
- Base

ILLUSTRATION: SOL 90, ALAMY X1, GETTY X1, ISTOCK X4

**THE GLOVES ARE ON**
The Queensberry Rules also outlawed the use of spring-enhanced footwear

# WHO LAID DOWN THE RULES OF BOXING?

⊚ They might be known as the Queensbury Rules, but the laws that largely govern boxing weren't actually drawn up by the man who gave his name to them. The 23-year-old 9th Marquis of Queensbury merely endorsed the code drafted by John Graham Chambers, a Welsh sporting polymath who also rowed in the Boat Race, staged the FA Cup Final and pioneered national championships in a variety of sports.

As well as including the first mention of the mandatory use of boxing gloves, the Queensbury Rules also determined that, among other restrictions, no wrestling was allowed, shoes with springs were outlawed, and rounds should last three minutes with a minute's rest between. Instituted to promote fair play, they also declared that "a man on one knee is considered down and if struck is entitled to the stakes". The rules were adopted in the US and Canada 22 years later, leading to a global standardisation of fight regulations.

# What are the origins of Christmas pantomime?

🎯 The peculiarly English-born Christmas pantomime has its beginnings in the 18th century. In the 1720s, entertainments heavily influenced by the Italian *commedia dell'arte* became increasingly popular thanks to their crowd-pleasing mix of humour, mime, spectacle and dance. Disliking the genre but unwilling to forego the profits, in the 1750s actor and theatre manager David Garrick limited pantomime performances in Drury Lane to the festive season. By the early 19th century, these "grotesque performances" were a well-established part of Christmas. The Victorian era saw harlequinade characters replaced by the cross-dressing dame and principal boy – as well as Italian-inspired tales being supplanted by English folklore – but the association with Christmas remains as strong as ever. Oh yes it does!

**DAME FOR A LAUGH**
Early pantomime was strongly influenced by Italian theatrical traditions

The world's oldest football was found behind panelling in Stirling Castle, and may have belonged to Mary, Queen of Scots

## WHAT'S THE EARLIEST RECORD OF A BALL BEING KICKED IN ENGLAND?

🎯 More than 500 years before William Webb Ellis would inadvertently invent the game of rugby – and a further four decades before the Football Association was founded – the first recorded evidence of a ball being kicked in England dates from 1280. The report focuses on a game played in Ulgham, in Northumberland, the noteworthy incident of which involved the death of a player, who ran onto an opponent's dagger. These rudimentary ball games carried with them plenty of controversy and, in 1314, the Lord Mayor of London issued a decree banning such sports: "For as much as there is great noise in the city caused by hustling over large foot balls in the fields of the public from which many evils might arise which God forbid: we command and forbid on behalf of the King, on pain of imprisonment, such game to be used in the city in the future."

# WHO CHOSE TO TURN DOWN THE BEATLES?

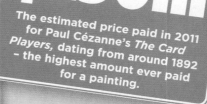

## $250m
The estimated price paid in 2011 for Paul Cézanne's *The Card Players*, dating from around 1892 – the highest amount ever paid for a painting.

🎯 Despite having sold over a billion units worldwide (according to EMI Records) – The Beatles' musical journey nearly ended before it began, when the Fab Four were turned down by no less than five record companies. Columbia, Pye, Philips, Oriole and Decca all declined to sign the group, with Decca's Dick Rowe reportedly declaring "guitar groups are on the way out". How wrong he was.

Nipper the dog only achieved his fame posthumously

## Was the **HMV dog** a real dog?

◎ Nipper was a terrier from Bristol who, three years after his death in 1895, had his portrait posthumously painted by his last owner. The painting showed the mutt inquisitively looking into a gramophone horn, as if listening intently to the music being played. The painting was sold to The Gramophone Company who used it as the trademark of their His Master's Voice record label. Nipper remained part of the HMV logo for more than 100 years.

### DID YOU KNOW?
**STARKERS SPRINTERS**
Although the Olympics were invented long before, the first *recorded* Games were in 776 BC. They featured one event – a sprint over 192m, which had to be run naked. The winner was a cook named Coroebus. As his prize, he was presented with an olive branch.

# WHEN DID WOMEN START COMPETING IN **THE OLYMPICS**?

◎ The original Olympic Games in Ancient Greece were all-male affairs and the introduction of the modern Games in 1896, held in Athens, were no different. At the very next Games four years later in Paris, however, women were able to take part, albeit in a limited capacity. Of the 997 athletes, just 22 were women, competing in five sports: tennis, sailing, croquet, equestrian and golf.

Throughout the 20th century, women's involvement in the Olympics increased. Since 1991, all new sports joining the programme are obliged to include women's events and London 2012 saw every participating country fielding female athletes for the first time.

## WAS HORNBLOWER BASED ON A REAL NAVAL OFFICER?

◎ Cecil Louis Troughton Smith – better known as CS Forester – used to spend hours engrossed in the early 19th century periodical *Naval Chronicle*, inspiring him to create Admiral Viscount Horatio Hornblower of Smallbridge. Hornblower's life was not based on one man, but drew its inspiration from the amalgamated adventures of many officers. Their exploits filled 12 novels, transforming a young, seasick rookie into the battle-scarred Admiral of the Fleet. Forester had no need to embellish the stories – he recounts that, if anything, they were toned down.

**HORATIO THE HERO**
The Hornblower stories were turned into a television series, starring Ioan Grufford (left)

# Who was the **Mona Lisa**?

◎ Commissioned around 1503, Leonardo da Vinci's 'Mona Lisa' is perhaps the most famous portrait in the world. With the artist himself making no mention of the work in his writings, a string of possible sitters have since been identified – including, bizarrely, da Vinci himself in drag – but it seems likely to immortalise Lisa del Giocondo (née Gherardini), the wife of a Florentine cloth merchant.

Although not conclusive, details about the suspected family and the painting itself offer some clues. At around the time the painting was commissioned, the Giocondos were a middle-class and aspiring couple celebrating the purchase of their own house and the arrival of a son – both events worth commemorating. The painting's alternative title, 'La Gioconda', may even allude to both the model and her famous expression, being not only the feminine form of Lisa's married name but translated roughly as 'the happy one'.

It has been mooted that the Mona Lisa was actually Leonardo da Vinci in drag!

ALAMY X1, GETTY X5, REX X1

# DID WORLD WAR I STOP FOR THE FOOTY?

The idea that, at the first Christmas of World War I, the two sides laid down their weapons and embarked on an impromptu game of football is an irresistible one. And there is a fair amount of testimony confirming that such events did spring up along the Western Front. One particular account, made later in the participant's life, reveals a match between a Cheshire regiment and the Germans: "Everybody seemed to be enjoying themselves. There was no sort of ill-will between us." A witness at another encounter between German and Scottish

**A series of unofficial ceasefires took place along the Western Front at Christmas 1914 and may indeed have included the playing of football**

soldiers recalled how "a sudden friendship had been struck up, the truce of God had been called, and for the rest of Christmas Day not a shot was fired along our section." The peace was fleeting; the two warring sides re-engaged hostilities on Boxing Day.

## DID YOU KNOW?

### FILLING A STADIUM

The word 'stadium' comes from 'stadion', an Ancient Greek unit of length. A stadion, measuring around 192 metres, was used to refer to a sprint race – the distance was calculated as being 600 times the length of the foot of Greek hero Heracles.

## WHAT WAS THE FIRST OPERA?

In 1598, Italian composer Jacopo Peri had the idea of putting on a musical play in which every single line was sung and the orchestra played throughout. The words were written by Ottavio Rinuccini, inspired by the story of Daphne and Apollo, and the work was named *La Dafne*. Peri called the show an 'opera', meaning simply 'piece of work'. The idea caught on and, soon, operas were being performed across Italy and, from around 1650, Europe.

# Did people have to **pay to go see gladiators** fight in Ancient Rome?

The Roman games of gladiatorial combat and animal hunts were great spectacles put on by senators, businessmen and, later, solely by emperors, in order to win the affection and favour of the masses. From the importation and feeding of exotic animals to the maintenance of warrior gladiators, the cost of laying on such events was immense.

But the hosts understood that the masses required entertainment to distract them from the grinding realities of life. The inaugural games at the Colosseum, for example, lasted for 100 days in AD 80, and were entirely paid for by Emperor Titus. All tickets were freely allocated (by lottery) to the citizens of Rome. The nature of the audience was strictly regulated, though, with the best seats in the house going to the wealthy and the upper classes.

**PUBLIC SERVICE**
Thousands of Romans were invited to watch the drama of the games

# GRAPHIC HISTORY
### Record-breakers of track and field

# WHAT ARE THE GREATEST RECORDS IN ATHLETICS?

### ROGER'S 'IMPOSSIBLE' MILE
On a blustery evening in Oxford in May 1954, a junior doctor called Roger Bannister set an awesome world record (WR), running a mile in **3 minutes and 59.4 seconds**. In doing so, the Brit crossed the four-minute threshold, which many **experts had believed to be impossible**, and inspiring countless other athletes.

## 100 YEARS OF 100M

Chipping away at the milliseconds for a century, this selection of record-breakers will be remembered as the fastest men on the planet...

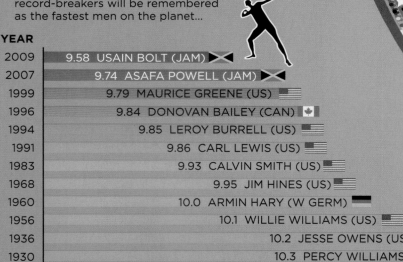

| YEAR | | |
|---|---|---|
| 2009 | 9.58 USAIN BOLT (JAM) | |
| 2007 | 9.74 ASAFA POWELL (JAM) | |
| 1999 | 9.79 MAURICE GREENE (US) | |
| 1996 | 9.84 DONOVAN BAILEY (CAN) | |
| 1994 | 9.85 LEROY BURRELL (US) | |
| 1991 | 9.86 CARL LEWIS (US) | |
| 1983 | 9.93 CALVIN SMITH (US) | |
| 1968 | 9.95 JIM HINES (US) | |
| 1960 | 10.0 ARMIN HARY (W GERM) | |
| 1956 | 10.1 WILLIE WILLIAMS (US) | |
| 1936 | 10.2 JESSE OWENS (US) | |
| 1930 | 10.3 PERCY WILLIAMS (CAN) | |
| 1921 | 10.4 CHARLIE PADDOCK (US) | |
| 1912 | 10.6 DONALD LIPPINCOTT (US) | |

9 | 9.1 | 9.2 | 9.3 | 9.4 | 9.5 | 9.6 | 9.7 | 9.8 | 9.9 | 10 | 10.1 | 10.2 | 10.3 | 10.4 | 10.5 | 10.6

**RECORD SET (seconds)**

**RECORD** Hammer
**WHEN** 1896-1911

Irish-born US champion, John J Flanagan set **his 14th hammer WR** at the age of 41 years, 196 days – the oldest athletic record-breaker to date.

**RECORD** High jump
**WHERE** Mexico City Olympics
**WHEN** 1968

Using the '**Fosbury flop**' method, US athlete Dick Fosbury set a WR height of 2.24m and changed the high jump forever.

**RECORD** Marathon
**WHERE** Helsinki Olympics
**WHEN** 1952

Czech runner Emil Zátopek set an Olympic record of 2:23:3, even though it was his **first competitive attempt** at the distance.

**RECORD** Discus
**WHEN** 1976

In 1976, Russia's Faina Melnik broke the long-targeted **70-metre mark** in women's discus, setting her **11th WR** of 70.5m.

**150,000**

THE CAPACITY OF THE **LARGEST ATHLETICS STADIUM** IN THE WORLD – THE RUNGRADO 1ST OF MAY STADIUM IN **PYONGYANG, NORTH KOREA**, BUILT IN 1989.

**RECORD** 100m
**WHEN** 1988

US athlete Florence Griffith-Joyner ran a new **100m WR of 10.49** seconds at the US Olympic Trials. She also set a **200m WR of 21.34** seconds in the same year. Both still stand.

**RECORD** Shot put
**WHEN** 1953-59

After developing the 180°-turn, Parry O'Brien of the US **broke the shot put WR 16 times** between 1953-59, becoming the first to throw over 19m. His PB was 19.69m.

**RECORD** Javelin
**WHERE** Potsdam, East Germany
**WHEN** 1988

The **80m mark** was a big deal in **women's javelin**. Petra Felke of East Germany reached it in 1988, the last of four WRs.

**RECORD** Decathlon
**WHERE** Götzis Hypo-Meeting, Austria
**WHEN** 2001

Roman Sebrle of the Czech Republic was the **first to top 9,000 points**. At the 2012 Olympics, 8,869 points secured gold.

**RECORD** Long jump
**WHERE** Mexico City Olympics
**WHEN** 1968

US athlete Bob Beamon's leap of 8.90m smashed the **old WR by 55cm**, and stood for 23 years.

**RECORD** Triple jump
**WHERE** Gothenburg, World Championships
**WHEN** 1995

Brit Jonathan Edwards was the **first to clear 18m** and his WR of 18.29 still stands (today's top triplers reach around 17.9m).

**12**

THE NUMBER OF OLYMPIC MEDALS WON BY FINNISH ATHLETE PAAVO NURMI BETWEEN 1920-28. IT REMAINS THE **MOST MEDALS WON IN ATHLETICS**. NURMI ALSO ESTABLISHED **25 OFFICIAL RECORDS**, AT DISTANCES RANGING FROM 1,500M TO 20,000M.

**32**

THE **NUMBER OF YEARS** SINCE CZECH RUNNER JARMILA KRATOCHVÍLOVÁ SET THE WOMEN'S 800M WR OF 1:53.28. IT'S THE **LONGEST STANDING** TRACK-AND-FIELD RECORD.

# WHAT IS THE **OLDEST SONG**?

For as long as they've been speaking, human beings have been singing and making music. Yet, despite claims that songs from ancient civilisations have been recovered – found carved into walls or impressed into clay tablets – it is nearly impossible to reconstruct ancient lyrics and melodies. Arguably the earliest-known song from antiquity, with both melody and lyrics recorded intact, is the 'Epitaph of Seikilos', a funerary piece intended for voice and the string instrument, the lyre. It survived and, immortalised in an engraving from the first century AD, contains these sobering lyrics:

*While you live, shine*
*Do not suffer anything at all*
*life exists only for a short while*
*and time demands its toll.*

**THE TUNE RUNES**
The oldest-known complete song was found engraved on a tombstone in Turkey

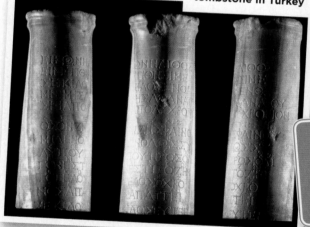

# Why do actors not refer to the Shakespeare play *Macbeth* by name?

Strictly speaking, the superstition states that actors must not utter the name 'Macbeth' in a theatre. If they do, the show currently being staged at that theatre will soon close. The only way to avoid the curse is apparently to leave the theatre, walk around it three times, spit over your left shoulder and curse. Others believe that merely spinning around on the spot three times and spitting will suffice.

It is usual, therefore, for theatrical folk to refer to 'the Scottish play', rather than name it. The most popular explanation is that Shakespeare used real spells revealed by real witches when writing the play. It's claimed the witches were so angry at having their secrets revealed that they cursed the play. However, there is little evidence for the superstition before the later 18th century, so its true origins remain a mystery.

**£750,000**
The cost of constructing the original Wembley Stadium, which opened in 1923

**TOIL AND TROUBLE**
Another way to undo the curse is by reciting lines from other Shakespeare plays

# WHEN DID THE ASHES BEGIN?

When the England cricket team lost to Australia in August 1882 at The Oval in south London, the manner of its shock defeat led to a spate of satirical obituaries lamenting the death of English cricket. The obituary that was published in *The Sporting Times* described how "the body will be cremated and the ashes taken to Australia". Ahead of the 1882-83 series to be held Down Under, England captain Ivo Bligh resolved to "regain those ashes". While in Australia – where he led England to a 2-1 victory in the three-match series – Bligh was presented with a terracotta urn, inside which were reportedly the ashes of a burnt wooden cricket bail. After Bligh's death in 1927, his widow presented the urn to Marylebone Cricket Club, which has displayed it at its Lord's ground ever since. The current Ashes urn is probably the world's smallest major sporting trophy. Believed to have previously been a perfume jar, even with its base it stands just 15cm high.

The Australian XI of 1882 featuring bowler Fred Spofforth (fourth from left) AKA 'The Demon' who was pivotal in the Aussie victory

## WHO FOUGHT?

Those sitting in the Colosseum could expect a host of different kinds of combat. A gladiator would either fight one-on-one against a man of equal strength and size or take on wild animals. Group battles were also common. There were many classes of gladiator, depending on their weapon of choice – such as swords, nets, tridents and spears – and the style of combat they specialised in, so a 'Thraex' wielded a short sword and shield while an 'Eques' fought on horseback. Although most fighting men were criminals, prisoners of war or slaves, some were volunteers seeking glory and riches.

## AFTER THE ROMANS

Following the downfall of the Roman Empire, the Colosseum was no longer used for gladiatorial games. It fell into disrepair as lightning and earthquakes caused severe damage, including the collapse of one side of the outer wall. Yet, greater damage was done by those stealing the rocks and marble to use on other construction sites. For centuries, the Colosseum became a quarry. Today, we can only get a hint of the majesty and awe-inspiring size of the original Colosseum.

### WHEN IN ROME
The Colosseum is one of Rome's most popular tourist attractions, with more than five million people visiting the ruins every year

### UP WITH THE GODS
As they weren't permitted in the lower tiers, women, the poorest men and slaves could only sit on the top level. This meant they would be some 100 metres away from the entertainment.

### UNDERGROUND MAZE
A network of tunnels – the *hypogeum* – ran beneath the arena floor. From there, pulley systems, platforms and trap doors allowed animals and gladiators to be raised for dramatic openings to contests.

### SECRET TUNNELS
There were tunnels leading from the *hypogeum* out of the Colosseum. Some were connected to nearby gladiator fighting schools, while another allowed the Emperor to avoid the crowds.

## THE GREATEST SPECTACLES

**WILD BEASTS**
It is thought 1 million animals died fighting either men or other creatures. Elephants, lions, bears, crocodiles, giraffes, rhinos and hippos were brought from around the known world.

**SEA BATTLES**
There are records from the early years of the Colosseum claiming that the arena was flooded with water so that historic naval battles could be reconstructed.

**CHRISTIAN MARTYRS?**
It has often been said that, as well as criminal executions, the Colosseum was the site of numerous martyrdoms of Christians, yet there is no evidence to support this.

# WHAT IS THIS MAN DELIVERING?

With a tray of hot, freshly-baked muffins perched on his head and a bell to announce his arrival, the muffin man used to be a common sight on British streets.

Like milk today, muffins were delivered door to door during the 19th and early 20th centuries. As a cheap food, they were eaten by many of Britain's poorer residents. A nursery rhyme about a muffin man "who lives on Drury Lane" was not only heard in British playgrounds, but was also a hit in the United States and the Netherlands.

# WHOSE FUNERAL IS THIS?

On 6 June 1989, in the searing heat of Iran, crowds of mourners reported to be in their millions pack the 25-mile route from Tehran to Behesht-e Zahra, graveyard of the dead of war and revolution.

Iran's beloved revolutionary leader, Ayatollah Ruhollah Khomeini, had died three days earlier, sparking a widespread and public outpouring of grief. At his funeral, fire fighters spray crowds with water to cool them, and mourners tear at the Ayatollah's robes for souvenirs. A number of people are crushed to death as chaos descends.

GETTY

# ARE THESE WOMEN WITCHES?

Enjoying afternoon tea in the Norfolk air in 1929 are four Sisters of the Hospital of Holy and Undivided Trinity, garbed in traditional Jacobean dress.

The Earl of Northampton, Henry Howard, built this almshouse in the early 17th century to provide shelter and support for 12 women from the local parish of Castle Rising. Sisters still attend prayers and services in witch-like hats and gowns with Howard's insignia emblazoned on them.

GETTY

PRESS ASSOCIATION IMA

# IS THIS THE ULTIMATE SOUVENIR?

It's April 1945 and World War II is in its final days. As the Allies march steadily towards Berlin, the Germans turn towards expensive and cumbersome railroad guns to mount a desperate defence. They're easily captured and make for an impressive souvenir snap, as seen in this photo of soldiers of the Seventh US Army posing with a massive 274mm gun that they've captured.

This wasn't even the largest gun developed by Hitler. The four-storey Schwerer Gustav had a goliath 30-metre barrel, weighed 1,350 tons and fired shells over tens of miles.

You may photocopy this form

# SUBSCRIPTION ORDER FORM

**Please complete the order form and send to:**
*FREEPOST IMMEDIATE MEDIA (please write in capitals)*

## UK DIRECT DEBIT

☐ I would like to subscribe to *History Revealed* magazine and pay £5 for my first 5 issues by Direct Debit*

## YOUR DETAILS (ESSENTIAL)

| Title | Forename | Surname |
|---|---|---|

Address

| Postcode | Home phone no |
|---|---|

Mobile tel no

Email

☐ **I wish to purchase a gift subscription**
(Please supply gift recipient's name and address on a separate sheet)

**Instructions to your Bank or Building Society to pay by Direct Debit**

DIRECT Debit

To: the Manager (Bank/Building Society)

Address

| | Postcode |
|---|---|

Name(s) of account holder(s)

| Bank/Building Society account number | Branch sort code |
|---|---|

Reference number (internal use only)

**Originator's identification number**

`7 1 0 6 4 4`

Please pay Immediate Media Co Bristol Ltd Debits from the account detailed in this instruction subject to the safeguards assured by the Direct Debit Guarantee. I understand that this instruction may remain with Immediate Media Co Bristol Ltd and, if so, details will be passed electronically to my Bank/Building Society.

| Signature | Date    /    / |
|---|---|

Banks and Building Societies may not accept Direct Debit mandates from some types of account

Your personal information will be used as set out in our Privacy Policy, which can be viewed at **www.immediate.co.uk/privacy-policy**.

## OTHER PAYMENT OPTIONS

☐ **UK by credit/ debit card or cheque** for just £43.85 for 13 issues **saving 25%**
☐ **Europe inc Eire** £59.00 for 13 issues
☐ **Rest of World** £62.00 for 13 issues

**CREDIT CARD DETAILS FORM**   Visa ☐   Mastercard ☐   Maestro ☐

Issue no ☐☐   Valid from ☐☐☐☐   Expiry date ☐☐☐☐

Signature                                        Date

☐ I enclose a cheque made payable to Immediate Media Co Ltd for £ _____

**OVERSEAS** Please complete the order form and send to:
*History Revealed*, PO Box 279, Sittingbourne, Kent ME9 8DF

*5 issues for £5 is available for UK subscribers and by Direct Debit only. After your first 5 issues, your subscription will continue at £19.99 every 6 issues saving 26% thereafter. If you cancel within 2 weeks of receiving your 4th issue, you will pay no more than £5. Your subscription will start with the next available issue. **Offer ends 31 December 2016.**

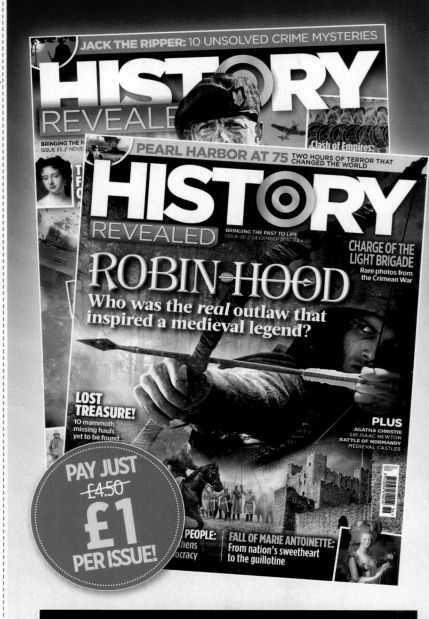

PAY JUST £4.50 **£1** PER ISSUE!

# DON'T MISS OUT – SUBSCRIBE TODAY...

■ **Pay just £5** for your first five issues*

■ **Continue your subscription** after your five issues at a low rate of **only £3.33 an issue**

■ **Free UK delivery** direct to your door

■ **Don't miss any of the amazing stories** coming up in the next issue of *History Revealed*